PREFACE

This book is a study of music associated with the English
cycle plays and uses, as source material, references to music
in the play texts and in the documents concerning production of
the drama. It is both descriptive and interpretive: lists of
songs, with texts and transcriptions of music that has survived,
and of instruments as well as a glossary of musical terms provide the basis of the volume; an introduction to the material
and commentaries on it supplement the lists and glossary. Extensive transcriptions of documents are not given, but complete
manuscript sources are cited. The bibliography presents works
(printed and manuscript) useful for the study of the subject of
music in the mystery plays. Four appendices--translations of
Latin texts, a list of liturgical music sources for the songs,
a table of all the plays and their music as it occurs, and a
concordance table--complete the volume.

The translations are attempts at plain prose style for
what is, frequently, allusive and ornate liturgical poetry; the
concordance, which correlates my references to the music in the
Chester plays taken from the Deimling-Matthews edition with the
Lumiansky-Mills edition of the cycle, is an acknowledgement of
the importance of this new version. I chose not to make it my
source, however, and decided as well to refer to the N-town
plays as the *Ludus Coventriae* because of the substantial tradi-
tions, scholarly and experiential, attached to the older term
and edition. Liturgical music has been assumed to have come
from the Sarum and York (for the York cycle) Uses because, of
course, England did not follow the Roman rite. The manuscript
sources (Gradual and Antiphoner) for these Uses are from the
thirteenth and fourteenth centuries, the printed sources (Missal, Breviary, Manual) from the sixteenth. Texts, all that the
printed books include, are not, however, different from those
in the manuscripts.

I wish to thank the archivists and librarians at Beverley,
Chester, Coventry, Lincoln, Norwich, and York, and Professors
Andrew Hughes and John Leyerle, all of whom enabled my initial
research to issue in a dissertation for the University of Toronto; Erindale College, University of Toronto, for a grant in aid
for publication of the photographs; the Hunterian Museum Library, University of Glasgow, and the Curators of the Bodleian
Library for permission to publish photographs of illuminations
containing depictions of musical instruments; Mrs. Jean Christie
for her cheerful and careful typing of my often indecipherable
manuscript; Professor J. R. O'Donnell, C. S. B., for assistance

with the Latin texts; Monte Schwarzwalder, for copying the
music; Professor Audrey Davidson for her keen eye and musical
sense; and especially Professor Clifford Davidson, general
editor of this series, whose patience, kindness, and encourage
ment have been a mainstay throughout the preparation of the
volume.

Music

in the English Mystery Plays

By JoAnna Dutka

Early Drama, Art, and Music
Reference Series, 2

MEDIEVAL INSTITUTE PUBLICATIONS
Western Michigan University
Kalamazoo, Michigan 49008
1980

SIGLA

Printed Texts

All references to the printed texts of the plays are to the following editions:

Chester	*The Chester Plays*, ed. Deimling and Matthews
Coventry	*Two Coventry Corpus Christi Plays*, ed. Hardin Craig
Ludus Coventriae	*Ludus Coventriae, or the Plaie called Corpus Christi*, ed. K. S. Block
Towneley	*The Towneley Plays*, ed. England and Pollard
York	*The York Plays*, ed. Lucy Toulmin Smith
Norwich	*Non-Cycle Plays and Fragments*, ed. Norman Davis

Manuscript Sources

References to manuscript sources of the plays are to:

B	Bodleian Library MS. 175, Chester Plays
D (Hm, Lumiansky-Mills)	Huntington Library MS. HM 2, Chester Plays
H	British Library MS. Harley 2124, Chester Plays
R	British Library MS. Harley 2013, Chester Plays
W (A, Lumiansky-Mills)	British Library MS. Add. 10,305, Chester Plays
C	Coventry Corporation MS. A 97, Weavers' Play
LC	British Library MS. Cotton Vespasian D. VIII, *Ludus Coventriae*

T	Huntington Library MS. HM 1, Towneley Plays
Y	British Library MS. Add. 35,290, York Plays

Liturgical Sources: Texts

Sarum Breviary	*Breviarium ad usum Sarum*, ed. Procter and Wordsworth
Sarum Missal	*The Sarum Missal*, ed. J. Wickham Legg
Sarum Manual	*Manuale ad usum . . . Sarisburiensis*, ed. A. Jefferies Collins
York Breviary	*Breviarium ad usum . . . Eboracensis*, ed. S. W. Lawley
York Missal	*Missale ad usum Eboracensis*, ed. W. G. Henderson
York Manual	*Manuale et Processionale ad usum Eboracensis*, ed. W. G. Henderson

Liturgical Sources: Music

AS	*Antiphonale Sarisburiense*, facs. ed., W. H. Frere
GS	*Graduale Sarisburiense*, facs. ed., W. H Frere
YG	Bodleian Library MS. Lat. liturg. B. 5, York Gradual
YB	Bodleian Library MS. Gough liturg. 1, York Breviary

CONTENTS

PLATES

1. King David and Musicians. Glasgow, Hunterian Museum Library, MS. 229, fol. 21[v].

2. Musicians playing Flute, Nakers, Bagpipe. Oxford, Bodleian Library, MS. Bodley 264, fol. 123[r].

3. Musicians playing Tabor and Flute, Psaltery, Fiddle, Trumpet. Oxford, Bodleian Library, MS. Ashmole 1523, fol. 99[r].

4. Angel Musicians. Oxford, Bodleian Library, MS. Douce 144, fol. 23[r].

5. Huntsman blowing horn. Oxford, Bodleian Library, MS.
Douce 219-20, fol. 49^r.

6. Angels with horns. Oxford, Bodleian Library, MS. Douce
180, p. 23.

I. INTRODUCTION

The surviving mystery plays of late medieval England contain songs, allusions to music, and directions for its performance, but these have received, for the most part, inadequate notice, since scholars who have dealt with this subject have concerned themselves only with the printed texts, not the original sources.[1] Others, remarking that the plays are not sung but spoken, and that they are not musical drama but include music in the drama, have tended to treat the music as merely incidental: that is, as background, as an interruption of the action, or as spectacular device.[2]

In my view, music in these cycle plays is essential to the production, and it is deliberately included for its dramatic utility as well as for its beauty. Moreover, it possesses great interest for the historian concerned with musical tastes and attitudes to music of non-courtly English society in the period from the late fourteenth century, when records of the plays' production are first found, to the last quarter of the sixteenth, when their final performances took place. In addition, the use of this music illustrates most strikingly the historical continuity of English dramatic practice throughout the late Middle Ages.

Accordingly, this volume sets out the results of a study of the types of music performed, of its functions within the plays, and of the contemporary records that give details of performance.[3]

The records are, in the main, the prosaic reckonings of city and guild inventories and expenses. In them, the requirements for equipping a pageant--the costumes, actors, and the contributors and helpers--are listed in diverse ways: some items are filled with lavish description, others are terse and tantalizingly compressed. They all, however, make plain the actual involvement of townspeople in the setting forth of the cycle plays and provide a context for the plays themselves. Payments to minstrels, singers, and other musicians as well as to persons whose roles require singing reveal details of the hiring of musicians and the wages paid them, the renting of instruments, and the type of music performed.

The external evidence of account books and other documents recording the expenses incurred by the play-producing craft guilds demonstrates clearly, moreover, that far more music was used in the plays than the texts actually indicate. This body of information reveals payments for songs, musicians, and instruments not mentioned in the texts. In Chester, four choirboys are hired for songs not given in the manuscripts of the Painters' play of the Shepherds, and the "whistles" provided for them suggest that the simple tunes played by the children would have allowed still more music in the pageant.[4] The Blacksmiths' Purification play has additional singers where the text calls for only one solo song: boy choristers, conducts, and minstrels are hired although they seemingly have no function within the action.[5] The text of the play of the Entry into Jerusalem at Chester requires no minstrels, but the Cordwainers hire them, and again the Cathedral supplies boys to sing.[6] The Precentor of the Cathedral is paid for songs, presumably new ones composed for the Smiths, and the Cathedral organist performs on the regals at least once.[7]

Coventry's guild accounts reveal less close cooperation between the Companies and the local churches than Chester's. The clerks hired as singers in the Coventry plays seem to have contributed only their voices,[8] whereas in Chester the Cathedral singing-men and boys sing, play instruments, and compose songs. On the other hand, although Chester records the payment of waits only once,[9] the Coventry Smiths, Drapers, Cappers, and Weavers all make use of the civic musicians over the whole period in which they produced pageants.[10] The Coventry Smiths' reception of four waits as brothers of the Company solely for the purpose of having a sure source of music for their play is unique, so far as I am aware.[11]

That the waits were regarded not merely as town functionaries but were expected to be musicians of great versatility is attested to by James Hewett's being hired by both the Drapers and Weavers for the same year's performances, not to play the customary instruments of a wait--the shawm, sackbut, etc.--but to perform on the regals. In addition, like his fellow wait Thomas Nicolls, who contributed pricksong to the Cappers' and Drapers' pageants, Hewett was a composer; the text of his song for the Weavers still survives.[12]

What is known regarding the original songs composed for the plays is slight; the names of Nicolls, Hewett, and the Norwich priest, Stephen Prewett,[13] are the only ones that

can definitely be associated with song-writing for the cycles.
None of their music exists, and only the texts of Hewett's
and Prewett's songs remain. Nevertheless, it is clear that
when new songs in the vernacular were required for a production, local composers were employed, presumably because their
talents in this field were recognized and their songs were
well-received.

The accounts indicate not only that more music, both
instrumental and vocal, was performed in the mystery cycles
than the manuscripts of the plays reveal, but also that
music was used in certain plays which recent writers have
maintained could not, by their very nature, have included
songs. John Stevens states:

> 'Heaven is music', so at the crises in the
> drama when heaven actively intervenes, music
> too intervenes. Heaven does not intervene
> during the Passion, when the powers of darkness
> are working their will. This is why there is
> no music when Christ is crucified. . . . None
> of the major cycles, to repeat, has music in
> scenes between the Entry into Jerusalem and
> the Harrowing of Hell (which follows the Burial
> of Christ). These scenes include the Betrayal,
> the Trials, the Scourging, the Buffeting, and
> the Crucifixion.[14]

Nan Cooke Carpenter concludes that "music is entirely lacking
in scenes dramatizing the darker episodes in the life of
Jesus."[15]

It is indeed true that no directions for music are given
in any of the Passion Plays of the four cycles, and for these
plays at York and Wakefield no accounts exist that might
indicate musicians were hired. Yet, knowing that indications
in the play texts are not always truly indicative of the ways
in which the mysteries were performed, that many vernacular
lyrics on the Passion are contemporary with the plays, and
that the liturgy itself has a repertory of suitable music,
one must hesitate before accepting the judgment of Stevens
and Carpenter. Moreover the Smiths of Coventry produced one
of the Passion plays, probably, from the list of characters,
that of the Trial of Christ before Herod. If Sharp's and
Halliwell-Phillips' transcripts of that guild's records
are at all trustworthy, minstrels and waits were paid for
the performances and were received as members of the guild
on condition they perform on Corpus Christi day with the
pageant.

The value the producers of the plays placed on music is revealed by the sums given the waits and the choir members. Expenditure on musicians considered as a performing unit rather than individuals is exceeded only the amount given the chief actor in the play: in 1534, the Coventry Cappers paid Pilate 3s 8d; they paid the singers and minstrels 2 shillings, more than any other single character. The proportion could change: Simeon of the Coventry Weavers' play had a maximum wage of 3s 4d; the musicians in the same pageant received that sum in their best year, 1561. The Drapers far surpass the other crafts in payments for music: their singers, trumpeter, and regals-player were never paid less than 4 shillings, while the standard fee for the actor playing God was 3s 4d.

The proportion between the total sum paid to the acting troupe and that to the musicians tends to remain constant for the three Coventry guilds whose records give the information. Three musicians were paid approximately one-fifth as much as eight actors by the Weavers through the period 1525-79; the Cappers paid three musicians approximately one-eighth as much as fifteen actors through the period 1534-79; and the Drapers paid approximately a quarter as much to four musicians as to eighteen to twenty actors in the same years.

In Chester, similarly, the sums spent on music were greater than for any single actor; the Smiths, moreover, in their 1567 Account paid more to the singers and minstrels than they did to the rest of the cast as a whole. And in Norwich, the grocer playing regals received as much as the actor whose role included singing. When one considers the amount of music performed in relation to the length of a principal role, the payments to musicians reveal what its importance must have been.

Other comparisons can be made. The salaries paid the Coventry waits do not seem to have varied from 1548-50 to the 1580's:[16] each of the four men received one pound, six shillings, and eight pence per year, or less than a penny a day. The chief wait, the trumpeter, was paid 3s 4d, or 40d, by the Drapers for one day's work in their pageant, and James Hewett received from 4d to 20d for playing the regals. When the latter was hired by two guilds on the same day, he earned a minimum of 2s 8d, or 32d, for that single day's labor. A musician would be eager to perform in the mystery plays when the wages were so enticingly high, twenty to forty times his normal fee. It seems that the principle of supply and demand is in operation here. If a guild were not able to provide musicians from among its

own members, it would be obliged to compete in the matter
of wages with other guilds equally anxious to secure musicians.
The latter could only profit by such a situation.

The amounts the minstrels or singers were given from
year to year must have varied with the quantity of music they
performed, as no standard rates of pay by the guilds seem
applicable. If, however, the four surviving Doomsday plays
are typical examples of that pageant, the 3s 4d customarily
paid to the trumpeter in the Coventry version appears
exorbitant in relation to the actual playing he did; his
talents must have been remarkable, for the actor playing God,
presumably the chief role in the play, received the same sum.
It should be noted that in 1439 it was ordered in an act of
Leet that "They Trumpet schall haue the rule off the Whaytes,
and off hem be Cheffe,"[17] and as leader of the waits he could
probably command a higher wage in virtue of his position.
Still, his wages from the city were no greater than those of
his fellow waits; the Drapers must therefore have believed
his skill as an instrumentalist warranted such high payments.

The problem arises whether, in a city such as York or
Beverley which had a minstrel's guild, rates of pay were
established by the musicians themselves, or if, because their
numbers included waits who as civic employees were at the
command of the companies, they all, or only the waits,
received fees decided upon by the guilds they served.
Unfortunately, the minstrels' ordinances of neither city
give any indication.[18] In addition, no answer can be
suggested for the question whether musicians belonging to a
guild received higher fees than minstrels, non-guild members,
who were hired especially for performances at the plays.

A final problem which the records of the guilds do not
completely solve is whether or not the musicians acted in
the plays. The activities of minstrel and actor were not
remote: the waits of Beverley were paid their yearly wages
as *histriones* in 1464, 1467, 1470, and 1502/3.[19] The waits
of Norwich in 1576 "did come here unto this [Mayor's]
courte and Craved that they myght haue leve to playe comedies
and vpon Interludes & souche other places [plays?] and
tragedes which shall seme to them mete, which peticion by
the hole concent of this courte is graunted to them so saue
as they do not playe in the tyme of devine service and
sermones."[20] The minstrels of York were granted permission
in 1561 to produce the "pageant of herod Inquyryng of the iij
kyngs for the child Jesu somtyme brought forth by the late
Masons of the said citie."[21] Church musicians too were
actors, as at Chester where choirboys played shepherds, Mr.
White may have taken Simeon's role, and Thomas Ellam had a

part in the same Smiths' play. The records appear to
indicate nothing more, however, than these few instances
of such a double function. Yet one is reluctant to think
that the mended trumpets which belonged to the York Mercers
and the Coventry Drapers were merely properties, silent
copies of instruments actually played by an unseen musician
and not, after all, by the angel announcing Judgment.

Although the accounts must be used to supplement the
play texts in order to reveal how much music the cycles
contained, the texts themselves clearly show music's importance to the dramatic functions of the cycles. It is used
in conjunction with the three components of drama: to
delineate character, to establish setting, and to advance
action. Among the means by which characterization is
accomplished through the use of music is the performance of
a particular type of song to reveal to the audience the
character of the singer. The Chester Gossips stave off the
impending doom of the Flood not with prayer and supplication,
but with a drinking song expressing defiant sentiments and
carefree jollity (57.225-32 and n.).

A more subtle means of characterizing with song is
employed in the Second Shepherds' Play of the Towneley
cycle where the manner of singing, not the type of song,
discloses character. The shepherds sing to ward off
tedium and the weather:

> primus pastor.   lett me syng the tenory.
> ii us pastor.   And I the tryble so hye.
> iii us pastor.   Then the meyne fallys to me;
>   lett se how ye chauntt. (122.186-89)

The entrance of Mak the thief, however, is greeted with "Who
is that pypys so poore?" (122.195). Mak's later attempt
at a lullaby is dismissed with scorn: "hard I neuer none
crak / so clere out of toyne. . ." (131.477). "Good"
characters and expert singing, "bad" characters and unmusical
sounds seem linked.[22]

Music provides realism not only by disclosing character,
but also by indicating the setting of particular scenes. In
the Conception of Mary play from the *Ludus Coventriae*, Bishop
Ysakar performs the ritual of incensing the altar while the
sequence "Benedicta sit beata Trinitas" is sung. He and his
ministers conclude the scene with a benediction sung anti-
phonally, thus furthering the illusion that the setting is a
place of worship (65.72-66.90). The wedding of Joseph and
Mary supplies the playwright with another opportunity to link
music and a liturgical setting in the singing of the sequence

"Alma chorus," which was used for the English marriage service.[23] The funeral procession and burial of Mary take place while "Exiit Israel" (367.341-42) and "De terra" (370.425-26) from the liturgy of the dead are sung.[24] Thus, the religious events of the audience's daily life-- their churchgoing, marriages, funerals--are related to the action being represented before them by appropriate music that vividly establishes the ritual setting.

The problem of indicating different settings in plays that are continuous productions without scenic divisions is frequently resolved in the mysteries by having music mark changes in the place being depicted. The customary type of change in locality is that in which both setting and characters differ. The *Ludus Coventriae* Conception of Mary play makes use of this device in the shepherds' song, which ends their discussion with Joachim and moves the action back to Anne (69.186). In my opinion, the most dramatically ingenious use of music to divide scenes is in the Coventry Shepherds play. The chief events are common to all the cycles: the angels' song and announcement of the Nativity, the ensuing discussion by the shepherds, and the setting forth to Bethlehem. In the Coventry play, the shepherds sing as they go, and with the song's performance the scene shifts to Mary and Joseph and the birth of the Child (10.after 277). After the shepherds have worshipped Christ, they "syngith ageyne and goth forthe of the place; and the ij profettis cumyth in. . ." (12.after 331). The songs are given separately at the end of the play, but they are actually the two stanzas of the carol "As I out rode," the first sung as the shepherds come to worship, the second when they leave. This is a most effective device for emphasizing the importance of the scene, for the stanzas thus enclose the action of the shepherds' adoration of the Child, set it off, and accentuate it as something unique and quite wonderful.

The relationship between music and the action of the plays is established with as much proficiency as is shown by the preceding categories of character and setting. The Chester plays use music to represent a time interval: for Adam, expelled from Paradise, thirty years of earthly toil (37.421-36); for Noah, forty days adrift. Noah retreats into his ark when the rains begin:

> This window I will shut anon,
> And into my chamber will I gone
> till this water, so greate one,
> be slaked throughe [God's] mighte

> (Tunc Noe claudet fenestram Archae et per modicum
> spatium infra tectum cantent psalmum 'Save mee
> o God' et aperiens fenestram et respiciens).
> Now 40 days are fullie gone. . . .   (58.253-57)

Music is used to facilitate stage business: to begin or end
a play, to accompany entrances, exits, and processions within
a play as well as the spectacular stage effect of ascents
and descents by God and the angels to and from heaven.[25]   In
all these instances, the functions of music are valid and,
indeed, technically excellent. It must be remembered, none-
theless, that the manuscripts we possess are not exact and
true witnesses to the mysteries.[26] In any given production,
the ways in which music was used may have been as I have
described them, or they may not. Did, for example, every
ascent, descent, entrance, exit, play beginning, or play
ending have music? Most likely not: the demands of a particular play and performance, the finances available for
musicians in certain years, the constantly changing notions
of production--all these factors would ensure that the use of
music would not follow rigid patterns, but would be as var-
iable and as capable of revision as the texts themselves
apparently could be.

The uses of music as a structural element are comple-
mented by its employment to achieve dramatic effect. The
device of framing a scene by songs in order to emphasize it
has already been described. Coventry's "As I out rode" is
not the only song used in this manner. In the York Appearance
of Our Lady, the vision of Mary being assumed into heaven is
enclosed by two songs, "Surge proxima mea" and "Veni electa
mea," performed by the angels accompanying the Virgin. Even
within the scene, the same technique is used. The opening
song is followed by a lyrical passage spoken by the twelve
angels, each in turn, in which litany-like invocations
translate, paraphrase, and elaborate the texts of the songs.

      i Ang.   Rise, Marie, þou maiden and modir so milde.
     ii Ang.   Rise, lilly full lusty, þi luffe is full likand
    iii Ang.   Rise, chefteyne of chastite, in chering þi
                 childe
     iv Ang.   Rise, rose ripe redolent, in reste to be
                 reynand.
      v Ang.   Rise, douffe of þat domesman, all dedis is
                 demand.
     vi Ang.   Rise, turtour, tabernacle, and tempull full
                 trewe.

```
 vii Ang.   Rise, semely in sight, of þi sone to be
            semande.
viii Ang.   Rise, grathed full goodely in grace for to
            grewe.
  ix Ang.   Rise vppe þis stounde.
   x Ang.   Come, chosen childe!
  xi Ang.   Come Marie milde!
 xii Ang.   Come floure vnfiled!
viii Ang.   Come vppe to þe kyng to be crouned.
```

The last angel's words are followed by the song "Veni de libano"
(483.105-484.117). This double framing is exceptional and
quite extraordinary in its artistry.

Another episode made highly dramatic through the use of
music is in the Coventry Shearmen and Taylors' play. The
pathetic lullaby of the women creates a mood of frightened
tenderness which is abruptly shattered by the grim soldiers
who have come to murder the infants to whom the mothers sing.
Although the entrance of the women--"Here the wemen cum in
wythe there chyldur, syngyng them; and Mare and Josoff goth
awey cleyne" (29.after 829)--covers the exit of the Holy
Family, the song (32.1-18) functions less as a technical
device than as a means of establishing a mood to foreshadow
and to contrast with that of the following action.

Contemporary ideas about music and attitudes towards it
are revealed throughout the plays. Music is considered the
natural accompaniment to one's daily occupations (Chester,
141.216), and both joy and sorrow find their outlet in song.
Mary sings her "Magnificat" with "joifull mirth" (Chester,
107.67); Adam and Eve mourn, "Therfor owr handes we may
wrynge with most dullfull song," and sing "Wythe dolorous
sorowe" (Norwich, 10.88-90). Because of the association of
joy and song, heaven, which is a condition of perfect joy,
is the place where "myrthe and melody nevyr may mys"
(Ludus Coventriae, 375.56) and where the angels are constantly
making melody.[27] The angels' singing is of remarkable beauty:
Joseph describes it as "swete of toyn" (Towneley, 161.13)
and the Chester shepherd willingly acknowledges, "[Gabriel]
had a much better voyce then had I/ as in heaven all other
haue so" (149.417-18).

An additional characteristic of angelic song is noted in
the two Towneley Shepherds plays. In the first, the shepherds
comment:

```
     ij us pastor.  Now, by god that me boght/ it was
                    a mery song;
                 I dar say that he broght/ foure & twenty to
```

                    a long. . . .   (113.413-14)

Wonder at the rhythmic complexity of the angel's "Gloria" is
also expressed in the second play:

        ij us pastor.   Say, what was his song? / hard ye
                            not how he crakyd it?
                         Thre brefes to a long. /
        iii us pastor.   yee, mary,
                         he hakt it.
                         was no crochett wrong / nor no thyng
                            that lakt it. (137.656-58)

In contrast with the florid virtuosity of the heavenly
announcement is the style of the shepherds' own singing:
in three parts--tenor, mean, and treble (122.186-88)--and
"in syght" (116.502).[28] The difference between this
improvised, probably syllabic discant and the ornate,
technically complex melody of the angel creates a dramatic
contrast which therefore opposes by implication the supernatural character of the angel and the simple humanity of
the shepherds. Just as the nature of an angelic being is of
a different order from that of a human, so is his music in
its complexity and virtuosity symbolic of his supernatural
condition.
     The music of heaven has yet another quality: the capacity
for affecting its hearers according to their states of grace.
For Thomas, "þis mirthe and þis melody mengis my mode" (York,
484.123). Octavian exclaims after hearing the angel's
"Hec est ara celi":

            My members all it goeth among,
            Ioy and blis makes my hart strong,
            To hear this melodye. (Chester, 130.682-84)

Joseph responds to the "Gloria" in like manner: "This grett
solemnete/ Gretly amended hath my chere" (Coventry, 10.279-80),
and even Gartius, the most irreverent of the Chester shepherds,
is affected: "he sang also of a 'Deo'/ me thought that healed
my hart" (150.441-42).
     Music has, however, a different effect on the wicked.
To the evil princes in the *Ludus Coventriae* Assumption, the
combined angelic and human music at Mary's funeral is fright-
eningly ominous:

            sweche other noyse · herd I neuer er

> myn herte gynnth ogyl · and quake for fer. . . .
>
> (368.353-54)

The soldiers guarding Christ's tomb are completely over-
whelmed by his Resurrection:

> We wer so ferde downe ganne we falle,
> And dared for drede.
>
>   ·   ·   ·
>
> We herde never sen we were borne,
> Nor all oure faderes vs be-forne,
> Such melodie, mydday ne morne,
>   As was made þere. (York, 416.369-417.386)

Furthermore, in hell, the very sounds of music become per-
verted. The devil Rybald, in the Towneley Harrowing, calls
the "Salʋator mundi" of the saved souls "a dyn" and an
"vgly noyse" (296.90 and 95), and the call to Judgment is,
to the damned, "spytus" and "hydous" (Towneley, 368.41,
and York, 500.115). When the effects of music on its good
and evil hearers were so carefully distinguished by the
playwrights, it is disappointing that no stage directions
survive to describe what the music of hell was conceived
to be.

John Stevens believes that "the music of hell was, of
course, discord--'clamor vel sonitus materialis magnus'
(see Chester, p. 323,--Harrowing of Hell), i.e. probably
pots and pans."[29] In the first place, the Chester stage
direction does not refer to the music of hell, but to the
sudden appearance of Christ there and the breaking down of
the gates which stand shut against him. Secondly, to think
of discord necessitating the noise of pots and pans is
surely somewhat naive. In Marston's *The Malcontent*, the
opening scene of the second act has the direction, "The
vilest out of tune Musicke being heard," and John P. Cutts
notes, "cette musique horrible suggère l'atmosphère de
discorde qui règne dans le monde de la Cour. . . ."[30]

If the musicians of this play, printed in 1604, were
able to indicate evil by means of discordant music, why
would the musicians of a few decades earlier--men who are
participating in plays in which the notion of equating
wickedness and unpleasant music is common (Mak sings badly
because he is bad; the devils find music ugly)--have to
resort to the childish expedient of banging pots and pans
to represent hellish music? It was as easy to play or sing
out of tune in the sixteenth century as it was in the seven-
teenth, and other means of producing vile sounds, such as

the use of the tritone and the imperfecting of perfect con-
sonances, were equally available and would just as effectively grate on medieval ears. Discord would fittingly be
the music of hell and its creatures, for consonance and
harmony are manifestations of order and heaven is, of course,
perfect order, while hell is the contradiction of everything
divine. Although nowhere in the plays are the sounds of
hell and its devils described, one can safely assume they
are most effectively discordant and in complete contrast to
the celestial melodies.

Music is not, therefore, the prerogative of the angels
or the virtuous, but belongs as well, however distorted, to
the devil and his minions.

Although none of the play texts directs music to be
performed in the Passion sequences where evil appears to have
triumphed over goodness, the account books of some of the
guilds who produced those particular plays indicate that
music was used extensively and cannot be considered, as
Stevens and Carpenter believe, to have been restricted to
scenes of divine intervention.[31] Furthermore, to conclude
that "music is a heavenly thing. . . [and, hence] nowhere
. . . is there singing by . . . enemies of true religion"[32]
is to neglect the evidence from the Cornish plays where
devils and Christ's torturers sing, and from the Towneley
cycle where devils also sing.[33] Finally, the attitudes of
evil characters towards music reveal plainly that it is not
thought of as belonging solely to heavenly creatures.
Beautiful music may indeed be their prerogative, as Mak and
the shepherds bear clear witness, but music as an audible
phenomenon belongs to heaven, earth, and--in dissonance--
even hell.[34]

Such a use of music for symbolic purposes has ramifi-
cations in a closely connected area, for medieval writings
that consider the appearance and sound of musical instruments to represent or symbolize spiritual realities have
provided the opportunity for modern scholars to see a link
between the choice of instruments used in the mysteries and
their religious significance.

Edmund Bowles, for example, using medieval speculation
as a basis, discusses the symbolism of the instruments used
in continental mysteries, with some reference to English
plays,[35] and Nan Carpenter extends his descriptions to the
instruments mentioned in the cycles.[36] Thus, the Towneley
harp of David prefigures the cross of Christ; the organ of
the *Ludus Coventriae* is the house of God; bells are the
expression of God's word; and the wind which produces the
sound of the Judgment horns represents the breath of life.[37]

It is true, of course, that medieval theologians and philoso-
phers delighted in the play of ideas arising from symbolic
interpretations,[38] but one should note, in addition, that a
modern application of such meanings will not always fit the
actual circumstances.

To state, as Bowles and Carpenter do, that harps and
other soft-sounding stringed instruments as well as horns
were chosen for performance in the plays because of their
symbolic association with heaven and God does not agree with
the evidence of the Coventry Shearmen and Taylors' Play,
where "trompettis [and] viallis . . . bles the wakyng"
(19.538-39) of the tyrant Herod. That the instruments used
had a typological significance in the minds of the drama-
tists, producers, and audience may well have been so, but, as
the Coventry play demonstrates, typology was not and, indeed,
could not have been the sole basis for the inclusion of
instrumental music. Other factors--the availability of
instruments and people to play them, problems with acoustics
and sonorous effects of instruments in the open air, the
models available in sculpture and other art forms depict-
ing scenes similar to those in the plays--surely must also
have been involved.[39]

Didactic purposes, served possibly by the symbolism of
instruments, could have been aided as well by the songs of
the plays. It has been shown above that the words of a song
can perform dramatic functions; a lullaby, a drinking song,
a mournful song can characterize or establish a mood. The
words of a song can also reinforce the religious theme; at
Norwich they express grief at having offended God, and at
Coventry, joy over Christ's coming.[40] The meaning of these
songs in the vernacular would have been immediately grasped
by an audience, but the words to Latin songs which occur in
the plays often would not have been completely understood.
Though dramatically apt, their relevance would not always
have been readily apparent; in such instances a song's text
is frequently paraphrased or explained in the ensuing action.[41]

Could the music itself in any way emphasize the theme or
symbolize spiritual realities? Recognition of a melody, its
source and import, could create associations, but the texts
and music of the vernacular songs seem to be original; with
the possible exception of "troly loly," popular and hence
familiar songs do not seem to have been used. Familiar
melodies could have been set to new texts, however, and a
double association gained thereby, but no evidence of this
appears in the mysteries, although the practice is not uncommon in other contemporary plays.[42] Many of the melodies

of the Latin songs would have been familiar from religious events of daily life,[43] but some of the liturgical songs would be recognized only by those involved in the actual practice of the liturgy.

The ethical characteristics of the modes in which church music was composed are difficult, if not impossible, to categorize. Medieval theorists believed that each mode had its own *ethos*, but their attributions of mode and *ethos* differ greatly. For example, the effect of Mode VI, that on F, is described by Guido as "voluptuosus"; by Hermannus Contractus, "lamentabilis"; by John Cotton, "mimicos saltus faciens"; by John de Muris, "liberos saltus iocundi faciens."[43] It is not easy to see how "Ave regina celorum," written in Mode VI, can be considered either as possessing the varied characteristics attributed to its mode or as effecting such responses in its listeners. As we have seen, the power of music to move its hearers is clearly stated in the plays, but not on the basis of a predetermined quality in the music. The particular effect caused by the music depends largely, if not completely, on the spiritual disposition of the hearer, and, hence, the music can be affective only in proportion to his receptiveness.

How a character performs music or responds to it depends on the state of his soul, but whether or not he sings or plays hinges upon a number of more prosaic reasons. The resources necessary to have every character a maker of music would be far beyond the capacity of a craft guild to supply; England may have been a nest of singing birds, but most guilds probably were not. Moreover, if music, as I have tried to show, was considered to be functional, it would be kept within the limits of its use, not extended unnecessarily. In addition, a ready source of apt vernacular songs was probably not always available to most towns producing the cycles. Liturgical songs could not have been sung by a Herod or a Pilate, the themes of popular carols and other forms would not always suit the action of the plays, and professional songwriters, finding better markets for their talents in London and around the Court, were not plentiful in the provinces.[44] Thus, any character could sing; that he does or does not depends on practical, dramatic reasons rather than abstract, pseudo-religious ones.

Concepts of music seem, therefore, to have been rather less important to the playwrights than the practical application, the use of music. In its use, however, a shrewd understanding of the emotional impact of music can be observed at work--an understanding of the power and beauty of music, and of the significance of each of these aspects.

The preceding pages have indicated some of the many
functions music performs in the mysteries for the purposes
of dramatic effect, symbolism, internal unity, and stage-
craft. As well, the communal character of the productions
has been demonstrated by the records of the hiring of local
musicians, the choir members, organists, town waits,
minstrels.[45] The value placed on the music that all these
members of the community perform is illustrated in economic
terms by the high fees paid them, and in dramatic terms by
the suitability of the music chosen. The songs and instrumental pieces are relevant to the themes, actions, and
characters presented; the music itself, where borrowed from
the liturgy, exercises in its style a unifying effect on
the cycle as a whole; and vernacular songs and those familiar
from the ritual provide a certain measure of contemporaneity.
Music thus links the divine history being played out with
the everyday world of the audience and establishes a bridge
between religious ceremony and dramatic entertainment.

Music cannot be regarded, therefore, as subsidiary to
the other elements making up the plays--the physical means
whereby the plays are presented to an audience--but as
integral to the total dramatic statement and as equally
important to the producers and viewers as costumes and
pageant wagons. Moreover, the remarkable consistency in
the use made of music from town to town, as revealed by the
play texts, and the basically conservative retention of
these practices, as revealed by the accounts, indicates that
the conception of music in the mystery plays was part of a
dramatic tradition that lasted as long as the plays themselves.

This is clearly evidenced in the fifteenth-century
manuscript of the York cycle, where one-third of the directions for music are in the hand of a sixteenth-century
reviser whose suggestions do not differ from the titles
and uses in the other cycles. In addition, the same episodes in different cycles--such as the Resurrection and
Ascension sequences--are presented with the same music.
Even where a given dramatic situation would surely seem to
call for varying musical practice over a lengthy period of
time, the accounts reveal that the same expenses for the
same kinds of music are recorded year after year. The
plays are a continuing tradition, subject to variation and
revision but essentially constant, and the music they contain
consistently reflects this stability. Vernacular songs and
methods of performance might well have changed, but the
musical core of the plays, the songs from the liturgy, and
the functions of all the music remained the same until the

final suppression of the mysteries.

The playwrights and producers thus recognized the value of music as an aesthetic and structural element in their plays. Their utilization of it illustrates how music as both art form and social function was united with drama to create a vital and significant expression of medieval English life.

II. INDEX OF SONGS IN THE MYSTERY PLAYS

The information for each Latin song is given in the following order:

a. Incipit
b. Text
c. Cycle and play
d. Manuscript sources
e. Liturgical type
f. Liturgical source for text

The incipits are exactly as in the editions of the plays; the complete texts, on the other hand, are given as they are printed in the liturgical sources except where a source has not been located.

Each English song is treated in the following manner:

a. Incipit
b. Complete text
c. Cycle and play
d. Manuscript source
e. Editions or, where applicable, a reference to the *Index of Middle English Verse*

The incipits and texts are taken from the editions of the plays. Because the liturgical texts of the Latin songs may or may not have been sung as plainsong, transcriptions of the liturgical melodies are not included here. The York, Coventry, and Chester songs with music are, however, transcribed in their appropriate places in this index, with York and Chester in Part A, and Coventry in Part B. The editorial principles I have observed are as follows:

Prefatory staves show the original clefs and the first few notes of the source. The reductions are indicated above the treble stave at the opening of each song.

Key and time signatures have been regularized; barring is in accordance with the time signature given. Where necessary, odd measures have been inserted and the time change indicated. Double bars at the end of sections and songs

replace the single and sometime triple strokes that are
given in the sources. The last notes have generally been
replaced by a conventional half-note with fermata.

Colored notes are shown by ⌐   ¬ (except for
sixteenth notes), ligatures by ⌐   ¬. Editorial
additions are indicated by square brackets or, in the
case of accidentals, are placed above the notes to which
they refer, and emendations are shown by asterisks except
for the Coventry songs, where the variants among the stanzas
as reproduced by Sharp are given on a separate page.

The texts are as given in the sources, with punctuation, word division, and capitalization modernized. Manuscript contractions and abbreviations have been silently
expanded.

The York texts follow the words of the lower voice
since those of the upper voice are not always complete,
the Coventry texts those of the highest voice. Where the
latter has an inferior reading, I have corrected it from
the other voices.

All corrections and emendations of the Coventry
sources are listed separately; spelling variants are not
recorded. All words in square brackets are editorial.
Finally, the underlay is an attempt to produce a singable
version.

A.   LATIN SONGS

1.   a.   Accipite spiritum sanctum

     b.   Accipite spiritum sanctum quorum remiseritis
          peccata remittantur eis [Chester: eius].

     c.   Chester, Descent of the Holy Spirit, p. 381, after
          line 238

     d.   B, fol. 147^r
          D, fol. 125^r
          H, fol. 113^r
          R, omitted
          W, fol. 143^r

     e.   Antiphon

f.   Sarum Breviary, I, mviii

2. a.   Adiutorium nostrum

    b.   Adiutorium nostrum in nomine domini
            Qui fecit celum et terram
         Sit nomen domini benedictum
            Ex hoc nunc et usque in seculum
         Benedicat vos diuina maiestas et vna deitas
         + Pater + et filius + et spiritus sanctus
            Amen

    c.   *Ludus Coventriae*, Conception of Mary, p. 66,
         lines 85-90

    d.   LC, fol. 39^V

    e.   A variation of the common form of benediction given
         at the end of a ceremony.

    f.   *Benedictional of Archbishop Robert of Canterbury,* ed.
         H. A. Wilson, Publications of the Henry Bradshaw
         Society, 24 (1902).

3. a.   Alma chorus

    b.   Alma chorus domini, nunc pangat nomina summi.
         Messias, Sother, Emanuel, Sabaoth, Adonay.
         Est unigenitus, via, vita, manus, homousyon,
         Principium, primogenitus, sapientia, virtus,
         Alpha, caput finisque simul vocitatur, et est oo.
         Fons et origo boni paraclytus ac mediator,
         Agnus, ovis, vitulus, serpens, aries, leo, vermis,
         Os, verbum, splendor, sol, gloria, lux et imago,
         Panis, flos, vitis, mons, janua, petra, lapisque,
         Angelus, et sponsus, pastorque, propheta, sacerdos,
         Athanatos, kyrios, theos, panton, crathon, et ysus,
         Salvificet nos: sit cui secla per omnia doxa.
         Amen.

    c.   *Ludus Coventriae*, Betrothal of Mary, p. 93, line
         334

    d.   LC, fol. 55^V

    e.   Sequence

    f.   Sarum Breviary, II, 236, and III, 618

4.   a.   Ascendo ad Patrem

    b.   Ascendo ad Patrem meum et Patrem vestrum, Deum meum et Deum vestrum. Alleluia. [Chester adds: Alleluia].

    c.1   Chester, Ascension, p. 367, after line 104
    c.2   Towneley, Ascension, p. 361, after line 253
    c.3   York, Ascension, p. 461, line 178, fn. 3

    d.1   B, fol. 141^v
           D, fol. 120^r
           H, fol. 107^v
           R, fol. 164^v
           W, fol. 138^v
    d.2   T, fol. 120^r
    d.3   Y, fol. 224^r

    e.1   Antiphon
    e.2   Respond
    e.3   Versicle and Response

    f.1   Sarum Breviary, I, dcccclxiii
           York Breviary, I, 480
    f.2   York Breviary, I, 481
    f.3   Sarum Breviary, I, dcccclxii and dcccclxv

5.   a.   Assumpta es [sic] Maria

    b.   Assumpta est Maria in celum: gaudent angeli et collaudantes benedicunt dominum.

    c.   *Ludus Coventriae*, Assumption, p. 373, line 494

    d.   LC, fol. 222^v

    e.1   Alleluia
    e.2   Antiphon

    f.1   Sarum Missal, 309
    f.2   Sarum Breviary, III, 698, 699, 700

6. a. Ave maria . . . sesena [sic]

    b. Ave maria gratia plena. Dominus tecum, virgo
        serena.
        Benedicta tu in mulieribus. Quae peperisti pacem
        hominibus, et angelis gloriam.
        Et benedictus fructus ventris tui. Qui coheredes
        ut essemus sui nos, fecit per gratiam.
        Per hoc autem ave: mundo tam suave, contra
        carnis jura,
        Genuisti prolem novum stella solem nova genitura.
        Tu parvi et magni leonis et agni, Salvatoris
        Christi templum extitisti sed virgo intacta.
        Tu floris et roris, panis et pastoris, virginum
        regina, rosa sine spina genitrix es facta.
        Tu civitas regis justiciae, tu mater es miseri-
        cordiae; Theophilum reformans gratiae, de lacu
        facis et miseriae.
        Ergo maris stella, verbi Dei cella et solis aurora,
        Paradisi porta. Per quam lux est orta, Natum
        tuum ora,
        Nos ut solvat a peccatis, et in regno claritatis
        quo lux lucet sedula collocet per secula. Amen.

    c. *Ludus Coventriae*, Annunciation, p. 108, after line
        340

    d. LC, fol. 66^r

    e. Sequence

    f. Sarum Breviary, II, 517

7. a. Ave regina celorum

    b. Ave regina celorum
        Ave domina angelorum
        Salve radix sancta
        Ex qua mundo lux est orta
        Ave gloriosa
        Super omnes speciosa
        Vale valde decora
        Et pro nobis semper Christum exora.

    c.1 *Ludus Coventriae*, Visitation, p. 122, line 36
    c.2 York, Death of Mary, p. 479, after line 194

d.1   LC, fol. 74^r
d.2   Y, fol. 223^r

e.   Antiphon

f.   Sarum Breviary, I, dcccxxvii and mclxix; III, 784
      York Breviary, I, 417, 493, 682

8. a.   Beatam me dicent

    b.   Beatam me dicent omnes generationes, quia fecit
         mihi Dominus [*Lud. Cov.*: omitted] magna qui
         potens est et sanctum nomen ejus.

    c.   *Ludus Coventriae*, Assumption, p. 365, lines 296-97

    d.   LC, fol, 219^r

    e.1 Respond
    e.2 Also a line from the Magnificat; see number 35
         below.

9. a.   Benedicta sit beata Trinitas

    b.   Benedicta sit beata Trinitas Deitas aeterna
              coaequalis gloria.
         Deus genitor, pariter Natus genitus cum sacro
              Pneumate permanens super omne quod extat.
         Quibus est una semper voluntas et a se discrepans
              haud unquam triplicata persona.
         Nam constat Deitas una non in tres Deos divisa
              quod fides fatetur a Christo orthodoxe dedita.
         Haec namque pellit delicta patriam cedit serenam:
              qua dulcem jubilant agmina symphoniam caelica.
         Altithroni vestigia imitantur stolis candidata.
         Operiunturque binas quas captant post secli
              discrimina.
         Et nos quos illustrat gratia Dei superaddemus
              nostra debita.
         Quatenus caterva caelica nobis maneat post funera
              socia.
         Ultimoque peracto discrimine possimus alto perfrui
              mox palaciis.
         Quo perspicua flagrat lux accensa constanti flamma,
              quae Deus est visio nostra et salus aeterna.

Angelorum quae illustrat fortiter pectora.
Ut in Christo solo sua defigant lumina.
Haec namque est illa sitis flagrans qua tunc sitient
animae sanctorum et corpora.
Cum fuerint data perpetua eis pro bonis a judice
praemia.

c.1 *Ludus Coventriae*, Conception of Mary, p. 65, after
line 72

c.2 *Ludus Coventriae,* Betrothal of Mary, p. 91, after
line 301

d.1 LC, fol. 39^r
d.2 LC, fol. 55^r

e. Sequence

f. Sarum Breviary, II, 502

10. a. Cantemus Domino

b. Cantemus Domino, gloriose enim honorificatus est,
equum et ascensorum projecit in mare. Adjutor et
protector factus est mihi Dominus in salutem.

c. York, Pharoah, p. 91, line 406

d. Y, fol. 43^r

e. Respond

f. York Breviary, I, 330

11. a. Christus resurgens

b. Christus resurgens ex [Chester: a] mortuis; jam
non moritur mors illi ultra non dominabitur [The
antiphon continues: quod enim vivit, vivit deo.
Alleluya, Alleluya].

c.1 Chester, Resurrection, p. 337, after line 153
c.2 Towneley, Resurrection, p. 313, after line 225
c.3 York, Resurrection, p. 406, after line 186, fn. 1

d.1 B, fol. 131^r

D, fol. 110$^\text{v}$
H, fol. 96$^\text{v}$
R, fol. 149$^\text{v}$
W, fol. 127$^\text{v}$
d.2   T, fol. 103$^\text{v}$
d.3   Y, fol. 202$^\text{r}$

e.1   Communion
e.2   Antiphon
e.3   Respond

f.1   Sarum Missal, 141
      York Missal, I, 131
f.2   Sarum Breviary, I, dcccvii
f.3   York Breviary, I, 415

12. a.   De terra plasmati me

     b.   De terra plasmati me et carnem [*Lud. Cov*: carne]
          induisti me: Redemptor meus domine resuscita me
          in novissimo die.

     c.   *Ludus Coventriae*, Assumption, p. 370, 425-26

     d.   LC, fol. 221$^\text{v}$

     e.   Antiphon

     f.   Sarum Manual, 158

13. a.   Dignus es domine

     b.   Dignus es domine deus noster, accipere gloriam et
          honorem et virtutem; quia tu creasti omnia, et
          propter voluntatem tuam erant et creata sunt:
          Salus Deo nostro qui sedet super thronum et Agno.
          Alleluia.

     c.   Chester, Fall of Lucifer, p. 12, after line 64

     d.   B, fol. 4$^\text{r}$
          D, missing
          H, fol. 1$^\text{v}$
          R, fol, 5$^\text{r}$
          W, fol. 2$^\text{r}$

e. Antiphon

f. Sarum Missal, 95
    Sarum Breviary, I, dcccxci

14. a. Ecce dominus ascendet

b. Ecce dominus ascendet super nubem levem et
    ingredietur egiptum, et movebuntur simulacra
    Egipti a facie Domini exercituum.

c. Chester, Massacre of the Innocents, p. 196, after
    line 264, and p. 197, after line 288

d. B, fol. 75^v
    D, fol. 52^v
    H, fol. 56^r
    R, fol. 82^v
    W, omitted

15. a. Ecce venio

b. Ecce venio quia in capite libri scriptum est de
    me vt facerem voluntatem tuam deus meus quia
    exultavit spiritus meus in deo salutari meo.

c. *Ludus Coventriae*, Assumption, p. 366, lines
    299-301

d. LC, fol. 219^r

16. a. Ego qui loquor

b. Ego qui loquor Iusticiam, et propugnator sum ad
    salvandum.

c. Chester, Ascension, p. 367, after line 104

d. B, fol. 141^v
    D, fol. 120^v
    H, fol. 108^r
    R, fol. 164^v
    W, fol. 138^v

17. a. Et vestimenta tua

    b. Et vestimenta tua sicut Calcantium in Torculari.

    c. Chester, Ascension, p. 367, after line 104

    d. B, fol. 141^v
        D, fol. 120^v
        H, fol. 108^r
        R, fol. 164^v
        W, fol. 138^v

18. a. Ex Egipto vocavi

    b. Ex Egipto vocavi filium meum, veniet ut salvet
        populum suum [Chester: ut salvum faciet populum
        meum].

    c. Chester, Massacre of the Innocents, p. 205, after
        line 496

    d. B, fol. 78^v
        D, fol. 65^r
        H, fol. 58^r
        R, fol. 86^r
        W, fol. 73^v

    e. Antiphon

    f. Sarum Breviary, I, lxvii

19. a. Exaltare domine

    b. Exaltare domine, in virtute tua, cantabimus et
        psallemus, virtutes tuas. Alleluia.

    c. Chester, Ascension, p. 369, after line 152

    d. B, fol. 142^v
        D, fol. 121^r
        H, fol. 108^v
        R, omitted
        W, omitted

    e.1 Antiphon

e.2 Respond
e.3 Verse and Response

f.1 Sarum Breviary, I, dcccclxvi
f.2 Sarum Breviary, I, dcccclxxi
f.3 Sarum Breviary, I, ccccxii, mclxxvii

20. a. Exiit Israel

b. In exitu [*Lud. Cov.*: exiit] Israel de egipto
domus iacob de populo barbaro. Alleluia. Facta
est iudea sanctificacio eius israel potestas
eius. Alleluia.

c. *Ludus Coventriae*, Assumption, p. 367, lines 341-42

d. LC, fol. 220^r

e.1 Alleluia
e.2 Psalm in the Burial Service

f.1 Sarum Missal, 196
f.2 Sarum Missal, 428 and 447

21. a. Exultet celum

b. Exultet caelum laudibus, resultet terra gaudiis
Archangelorum gloria sacra canunt solennia.
Vos secli justi judices, et vera mundi lumina:
Votis precamur cordium, audite preces supplicum.
Qui caelum verbo clauditis, serasque ejus
      solvitis:
Nos a peccatis omnibus solvite jussu, quaesumus.
Quorum praecepto subditur salus et languor omnium,
Sanate aegros moribus, nos reddentes virtutibus.
Ut cum judex advenerit Christus in fine seculi,
Nos sempiterni gaudii Faciat esse compotes.
Deo Patri sit gloria, ejusque soli Filio
Cum Spiritu Paraclito, et nunc et in perpetuum.
      Amen.

c. *Ludus Coventriae*, Conception of Mary, p. 68, after
line 146

d. LC, fol. 40^v

e. Hymn

f. Sarum Breviary, II, 368

22. a. Gaudete justi

b. Gaudete justi in Domino: rectos decet collaudatio.

c. Chester, Antichrist, p. 427, after line 730

d. B, fol. 165^r
    D, fol. 141^v
    H, fol. 130^v
    R, fol. 193^v
    W, fol. 161^r

e.1 Communion
e.2 Versicle and Response
e.3 Respond

f.1 Sarum Missal, 261, 268, 322, 342, 370
f.2 Sarum Breviary, II, 358 and 359
f.3 Sarum Breviary, II, 359

23. a. Gloria in excelsis Deo

b. Gloria in excelsis Deo, et in terra pax hominibus,
    bonae voluntatis. . . .

c.1 Chester, Shepherds, p. 147, after line 368
c.2 Coventry, Shearmen and Taylors' Play, p. 9, after
    line 263, and p. 10, after line 281
c.3 Ludus Coventriae, Shepherds, p. 148, after line 61
c.4 Towneley, Shepherds Plays, 1 and 2, p. 109, after
    line 295, and p. 136, after line 637
c.5 York, Shepherds, p. 120, line 58

d.1 B, fol. 56^r
    D, fol. 45^v
    H, fol. 42^r
    R, fol. 61^r
    W, fol. 51^r
d.2
d.3 LC, fol. 89^v
d.4 T, fols. 35^v and 45^r

d.5   Y, fol. 57^r

e.1   Gloria of the Mass
e.2   Antiphon
e.3   Versicle

f.1
f.2   Sarum Breviary, I, cxc
       York Breviary, I, 88
f.3   Sarum Breviary, I, clxxiv

BRITISH LIBRARY MS. HARLEY 2124, FOL. 42^r

24.   a.   Gloria laus et honor

     b. Gloria laus et honor tibi sit rex christe redemptor
         cui puerile decus prompsit osanna pium.
       Gloria laus. . . .
       Israel es tu rex davidis et inclita proles nomine
         qui in domini rex benedicte venis.
       Gloria laus. . . .
       Cetus in excelsis te laudat celitus omnis et
         mortalis homo et cuncta creata simul.
       Gloria laus. . . .
       Plebe Hebraea tibi cum palmis obvia venit.   Cum
         prece voto assumus hymnus ecce tibi.
       Gloria laus. . . .

    c.   *Ludus Coventriae*, Entry into Jerusalem, p. 241, after line 289

    d.   LC, fol. 145^r

    e.   Hymn

    f.   Sarum Missal, 96

25. a.   Gloria tibi Domine

    b.

    c.   *Ludus Coventriae*, Temptation, p. 199, after line 195

    d.   LC, fol. 119^r

    e.1 Response
    e.2 Doxology

    f.1 Sarum Manual, p. 38
    f.2 Sarum Breviary, I, cccxix, lxxii; II, 331, 234, 235

26. a.   Gloria tibi Trinitas

    b.   Gloria tibi Trinitas aequalis una Deitas et ante omnia saecula et nunc et in perpetuum.

    c.   Chester, Fall of Lucifer, p. 16, after line 192

    d.   B, fol. 5^v
           D, missing
           H, omitted
           R, fol. 7^r
           W, fol. 3^v

    e.   Antiphon

    f.   Sarum Breviary, I, mxlv; II, 49

27. a.   Hec est ara Dei caeli

    b.

c. Chester, Nativity, p. 130, after line 680

d. B, fol. 49^v
    D, fol. 40^v
    H, fol. 36^v
    R, fol. 54^r
    W, fol. 45^r

28. a. Hec est que nescivit

    b. Hec est que nescivit thorum in delicto [*Lud. Cov.*:
        delictis] habebit fructum [*Lud. Cov.*: requiem]
        in refectione [*Lud. Cov.*: respectu] animarum
        sanctarum

    c. *Ludus Coventriae*, Assumption, p. 365, lines 294-95

    d. LC, fol. 219^r

    e. Antiphon

    f. Sarum Breviary, II, 445

29. a. Hosanna filio David

    b. Hosanna filio David. Benedictus qui venit in nomine
        Domini. Rex Israel [Chester omits]. Hosanna in
        excelsis.

    c.1 Chester, Christ's Ministry, p. 257, after line 208
    c.2 York, Entry into Jerusalem, p. 210, after line 287,
         fn. 1

    d.1 B, fol. 100^r
         D, fol. 83^v
         H, fol. 73^r
         R, fol. 111^v
         W, fol. 94^r
    d.2 Y, fol. 109^v

    e. Antiphon

    f. Sarum Breviary, I, dcclx
        York Breviary, I, 367

30. a. Ista est speciosa

    b. Ista est speciosa inter filias Jerusalem sicut
vidistis eam plenam caritate et dilectione, sic
que in celum gaudens suscipitur et a dextris filii
in trono glorie collocatur.

    c. *Ludus Coventriae,* Assumption, p. 366, lines 317-19

    d. LC, fol. 219^V

31. a. Iste formosus

    b. Iste formosus in Stola sua, gradiens in multitudine
fortitudinis suae.

    c. Chester, Ascension, p. 367, after line 104

    d. B, fol. 141^V
D, fol. 120^V
H, fol. 107^V
R, fol. 164^V
W, fol. 138^V

32. a. Jesu corona virginum

    b. Jesu corona virginum, quem mater illa concepit:
Quae sola virgo parturit, haec vota clemens accipe.
Qui pascis inter lilia, septus choreis virginum:
Sponsas decorans gloria, sponsisque reddens praemia,
Quocunque pergis, virgines sequunter, atque laudibus
Post te canentes cursitant, hymnosque dulces
  personant.
Te deprecamur largius nostris adauge sensibus
Nescire prorsus omnia corruptionis vulnera.
Deo Patri sit gloria, ejusque soli Filio
Cum Spiritu Paraclyto, et nunc et in perpetuum.
  Amen.

    c. *Ludus Coventriae,* Mary in the Temple, p. 81, after
line 259

    d. LC, fol. 47^V

e.   Hymn

f.   Sarum Breviary, II, 448

33. a.   Laetamini in Domino

     b.   Laetamini in Domino et exultate justi: et gloriamini omnes recti corde.

     c.   Chester, Last Judgment, p. 445, after line 508

     d.   B, fol. 173^r
          D, fol. 147^v
          H, fol. 138^v
          R, fol. 210^v
          W, fol. 167^v

     e.1 Alleluia
     e.2 Offertory
     e.3 Respond
     e.4 Versicle and Response

     f.1 Sarum Missal, 367
     f.2 Sarum Missal, 241, 272, 278, 303, 316, 326, etc.
     f.3 Sarum Breviary, II, 407; III, 456
     f.4 Sarum Breviary, II, 396; III, 579

34. a.   Laus tibi cum gloria

     b.

     c.   York, Harrowing of Hell, p. 395, line 408

     d.   Y, fol. 199^v

35. a.   Magnificat anima mea

     b.   Magnificat anima mea dominum. . . .

     c.1 Chester, Nativity, p. 107, after line 64 and line 72
     c.2 York, Annunciation and Visitation, p. 101, after line 240

     d.1 B, fol. 41^v

D, fol. 33^v
H, fol. 29^v
R, fol. 45^r
W, omitted
d.2   Y, fol. 47^v

e.1   Canticle sung daily at Vespers
e.2   Antiphon

f.2   York Breviary, I, 903

36. a.   Mare vidit

b.   Mare vidit et fugit, jordanis conversus est retrorsum.

c.   *Ludus Coventriae*, Noah, p. 43, after line 253

d.   LC, fol. 25^v

e.   Psalm verse

f.   Sarum Breviary, II, 194

37. a.   Ne timeas Maria

b.   Ne timeas Maria, invenisti gratiam apud dominum.
     Ecce, concipies et paries filium.   Alleluia.

c.   York, Annunciation, p. 98, after line 152

d.   Y, fol. 46^r

e.   Antiphon

f.   York Breviary, I, 675; II, 234

38. a.   Non nobis Domine

b.   Non nobis Domine, non nobis; sed nomine tuo da
     gloriam.

c.   *Ludus Coventriae*, Noah, p. 43, after line 253

d.   LC, fol. 25^v

e. Psalm verse

f. Sarum Breviary, II, 194

39. a. Nunc dimittis

  b. Nunc dimittis servum tuum Domine in pace. . . .

  c.1 Chester, Purification, p. 211, after line 168
  c.2 *Ludus Coventriae*, Purification, p. 167, after line 146

  d.1 B, fol. 81^r
    D, fol. 67^v
    H, omitted
    R, fol. 89^v
    W, fol. 76^r
  d.2 LC, fol. 99^v

  e.1 Canticle of Simeon sung daily at Compline
  e.2 Tract
  e.3 Antiphon

  f.1
  f.2 Sarum Missal, p. 250
  f.3 Sarum Breviary, III, 143

40. a. Paratum cor meum

  b. Paratum cor meum deus paratum cor meum. Cantabo et psalmum dicam domino.

  c. *Ludus Coventriae*, Assumption, p. 365, lines 292-93.

  d. LC, fol. 219^r

  e. Respond

  f. Sarum Breviary, I, ccccxxvii

41. a. Pax vobis et non tardabit

  b.

c. Towneley, *Thomas of India*, p. 340, after lines 83 and 91

d. T, fol. 112^v

42. a. Que est ista

b. Que est ista que assendit de deserto deliciis affluens innixa super dilectum suum.

c. *Ludus Coventriae*, Assumption, p. 366, lines 315-16

d. LC, fol. 219^v

43. a. Quis est iste

b. Quis est iste qui venit de Edom, tinctis vestibus de Bosra?

c. Chester, Ascension, p. 367, after line 104

d. B, fol. 141^v
   D, fol. 120^v
   H, fol. 107^v
   R, fol. 164^v
   W, fol. 138^v

44. a. Salvator mundi

b. Salvator mundi Domine, qui nos salvasti hodie:
   In hac nocte nos protege, et salva omni tempore.
   Adesto nunc propitius, et parce supplicantibus:
   Tu dele nostra crimina, tu tenebras illumina.
   Ne mentem somnus opprimat, nec hostis nos surripiat:
   Nec ullis caro petimus, commaculetur sordibus.
   Te Reformator sensuum, votis precamur cordium:
   Ut puri castis mentibus, surgamus a cubilibus.
   Deo Patri sit gloria, ejusque soli Filio:
   Cum Spiritu Paraclito, et nunc et in perpetuum.   Amen.

c.1 Chester, *Last Judgment*, p. 445, after line 508
c.2 Towneley, *Harrowing of Hell*, p. 294, after line 44

d.1 B, fol. 173^r

         D, fol. 147^v
         H, fol. 138^v
         R, fol. 201^v
         W, fol. 167^v
d.2 T, fol. 97^v

e.   Hymn

f.   Sarum Breviary, II, 226

45. a.   Sanctus

   b.   Sanctus, sanctus, sanctus; Dominus Deus sabaoth.

   c.   York, Creation, p. 3, after line 40

   d.   Y, fol. 4^v

   e.1 Chant in the Ordinary of the Mass
   e.2 Also a line in the Te Deum; see below, No. 49A

46. a.   Simeon justus

   b.   Simeon justus et timoratus expectabat redemptionem
       Israel, et Spiritus sanctus erat in eo.

   c.   Towneley, Purification, p. 185, after line 132

   d.   T, fol. 61^v

   e.1 Antiphon
   e.2 Respond

   f.1 Sarum Breviary, III, 143, 144, 145

47. a.   Stella celi

   b.   Stella celi extirpavit
       que lactavit dominum
       Mortis pestem, quam plantavit
       Primus parens hominum.

       Ipsa stella nunc dignetur
       Sidera compescere,

Quorum bella plebum caedunt
Diro mortis ulcere.

c. *Ludus Coventriae*, Shepherds, p. 148, after line 77

d. LC, fol. 89^V

e. Antiphon

f. Cambridge, University Library, MS. Add. 6668, fols. 112^r-112^V [cf. Margaret Bent, "New and Little Known Fragments. . . ," *Journal of the American Musicological Society*, 21 (1968), 147, fn. 15].

48. a. Surge proxima mea

b. Surge proxima mea, columba mea, tabernaculum glorie, vasculum vite, templum celeste.

c. York, Appearance of Mary to Thomas, p. 483, after line 104, and p. 490, end of the play

d. Y, fols. 235^V and 241^r

BRITISH LIBRARY MS. ADDITIONAL 35,290, FOL. 235^V

* ◆ IS LEFT VOID IN MS.
INSTEAD OF BEING
COLORED RED.

40

SURGE

SUR

SUR

SUR

5

GE

GE

PRO-PE-RA ME

PRO-PE-RA ME

A CO-LUM-BA-

A CO-LUM-BA-

10

* ♩ IS C IN THE MANUSCRIPT.

42

49. a.   Te Deum

     b.   Te Deum laudamus, te Dominum confitemur. . . .

     c.1 Chester, Harrowing of Hell, p. 329, after line 260
     c.2 Towneley, Harrowing of Hell, p. 305, line 404
     c.3 Towneley, Judgment, p. 387, line 620
     c.4 York, Creation, p. 2, after line 24

     d.1 B, fol. 127^v
          D, fol. 108^r
          H, fol. 94^v
          R, fol. 146^r
          W, fol. 124^v
     d.2 T, fol. 101^r
     d.3 T, fol. 128^v
     d.4 Y, fol. 4^r

     e.   Hymn sung at the end of Matins

49A. a.   Tibi omnes angeli

b. Tibi omnes angeli, tibi celi et universae potestates,
    tibi cherubim et seraphim incessabili voce proclamant:
    Sanctus, sanctus, sanctus; Dominus Deus sabaoth.

c. *Ludus Coventriae*, Creation, p. 17, after line 39

d. LC, fol. 10^v

e. A section of the Te Deum

50. a. Torculor [sic] Calcavi solus

b. Torculor Calcavi solus, et de gentibus non est vir
    mecum.

c. Chester, Ascension, p. 367, after line 104

d. B, fol. 141^v
    D, fol. 120^v
    H, fol. 108^r
    R, fol. 164^v
    W, fol. 138^v

51. a. Veni creator spiritus

b. Veni creator spiritus, mentes tuorum visita
    Imple superna gratia, quae tu creasti, pectora.
    Qui paraclitus diceris, donum dei altissimi:
    Fons vivus, ignis, caritas, et spiritalis unctio.
    Tu septiformis munere, dextrae Dei tu digitus:
    Tu rite promissum Patris, sermone ditans guttura.
    Accende lumen sensibus, infunde amorem cordibus:
    Infirma nostri corporis virtute firmans perpetim.
    Hostem repellas longius, pacemque dones protinus:
    Ductore sic te praevio, vitemus omne noxium.
    Per te sciamus da Patrem, noscamus atque Filium:
    Te utriusque Spiritum credamus omni tempore.
    Sit laus Patri cum Filio, Sancto simul Paraclyto:
    Nobisque mittat Filius, carisma Sancti Spiritus.
    Amen.

c.1 Chester, Descent of the Holy Spirit, p. 376, after
     line 120
c.2 *Ludus Coventriae*, Betrothal of Mary, p. 82, line 115
c.3 York, Baptism of Christ, p. 177, after line 154

c.4 York, Temptation of Christ, p. 181, line 91, fn. 1
c.5 York, Descent of the Holy Spirit, p. 468, after line 96, fn. 1

d.1 B, fol. 145^v
    D, fol. 123^v
    H, fol. 111^r
    R, fol. 170^r
    W, fol. 142^v
d.2 LC, fol. 48^v
d.3 Y, fol. 88^v
d.4 Y, fol. 91^r
d.5 Y, fol. 227^v

e. Hymn

f. Sarum Breviary, I, mviii
    York Breviary, I, 503

52. a. Veni de libano

b. Veni de libano sponsa [Lud. Cov.: adds mea], veni coronaberis.

c.1 Ludus Coventriae, Assumption, p. 366, line 298
c.2 York, Appearance of Mary to Thomas, p. 484, after line 117

d.1 LC, fol. 219^r
d.2 Y, fols. 236^r and 241^v

BRITISH LIBRARY MS. ADDITIONAL 35,290, FOL. 236^r

BA____NO, SPON_____SA VE_____NI, CO___

BA____NO, SPON_____SA VE_____NI; CO___

_____ RO_____NA_____

_____ RO_____NA_____

DE_____RIS.]

BE_____RIS.

BRITISH LIBRARY MS. ADDITIONAL 35,290, FOL. 241ᵛ

VE _____

VE _____

* THE NEW MENSURATION SIGN O IS PLACED OVER THE TWO RESTS IN THE MANUSCRIPT.

** ♩ IS LEFT VOID IN THE MANUSCRIPT.

53. a.   Veni electa mea

b.   Veni [Lud. Cov.:   adds tu] electa mea et ponam in te
     thronum meum quia concupivit rex speciem tuam.

c.1 Ludus Coventriae, Assumption, p. 365, lines 290-91.
c.2 York, Appearance of Mary to Thomas, p. 487, after
     line 208

d.1 LC, fol. 219^r
d.2 Y, fols. 238^r and 241^v

e.1 Alleluia
e.2 Respond
e.3 Antiphon

f.1 Sarum Missal, 242, 292, 337, 350, 380, 390, fn. 3
     York Missal, II, 155
f.2 Sarum Breviary, II, 446
     York Breviary, II, 63 and 481
f.3 York Breviary, II, 77

48

BRITISH LIBRARY MS. ADDITIONAL 360,290, FOL. 238ʳ

* ◼ IS RED IN THE MANUSCRIPT

50

--A, ET PO- NAM IN TE TRO- NUM ME-

--A, ET PO- NAM IN TE_____TRO- NUM ME-

UM, QUI- A CON- CU- PI-- VIT REX SPE- CI-EM

UM, QUI- A CON-[CU-PI-VIT REX SPE- CI-EM] TU-

TU-' AM.]

AM.

*   ◆ IS ◆ IN THE MANUSCRIPT
** ◆ IS GIVEN AS ◆ IN THE MANUSCRIPT
*** THE MANUSCRIPT GIVES THREE RESTS HERE

BRITISH LIBRARY MS. ADDITIONAL 35,290, FOL. 241 V

54. a.   Venite benedicti

   b.   Venite benedicti patris mei: percipite regnum
     quod vobis paratum est ab origine mundi.

   c.   Chester, Late Banns, p. 8, line 184

   d.   B, fol. 2^V
     R, fol. 3^V

   e.1 Introit
   e.2 Antiphon

   f.1 Sarum Missal, 140
   f.2 Sarum Breviary, I, dlxxxviii

55. a.   Viri galilei, quid aspicitis

   b.   Viri galilei, quid aspicitis in celum hic Jesus qui
     assumptus est a vobis in celum sic veniet.   Alleluia

   c.   Chester, Ascension, p. 369, after line 152

   d.   B, fol. 142^V
     D, fol. 121^r
     H, fol. 108^V
     R, omitted
     W, omitted

   e.   Antiphon

   f.   Sarum Breviary, I, dcccclxii

B.   ENGLISH SONGS

1. a.   As I out rode

   b.   As I out rode this enderes night,
     Of three ioli sheppardes I saw a sight,
     And all a-bowte there fold a star shone bright;
        They sange terli terlow;
        So mereli the sheppards ther pipes can blow.

Doune from heaven, from heaven so hie,
Of angeles ther came a great companie,
With mirthe and ioy and great solemnitye,
    The sange terly terlow;
    So mereli the sheppards ther pipes can blow.

c.   Coventry, Pageant of the Shearmen and Taylors

d.   Thomas Sharp, *A Dissertation*, pp. 113-15, 118.

e.   *Index of Middle English Verse*, No. 112 and No. 3477

John P. Cutts, "The Second Coventry Carol. . . ," *Renaissance News*, 10 (1957), 3-8, includes an edition of text and music.

Richard L. Greene, "The Second Coventry Carol: A Correction," *Renaissance News*, 10 (1957), 142.

Richard Rastall, *Two Coventry Carols*, (Westleigh, Devon: Antico, 1973).

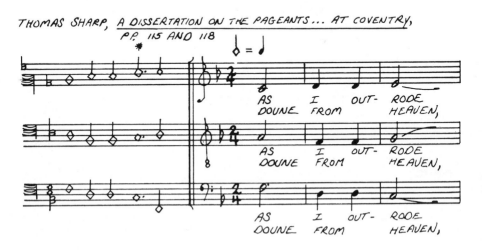

THOMAS SHARP, A DISSERTATION ON THE PAGEANTS... AT COVENTRY, P.P. 115 AND 118

* ♩. SHOULD BE ◇. IN THE ORIGINAL

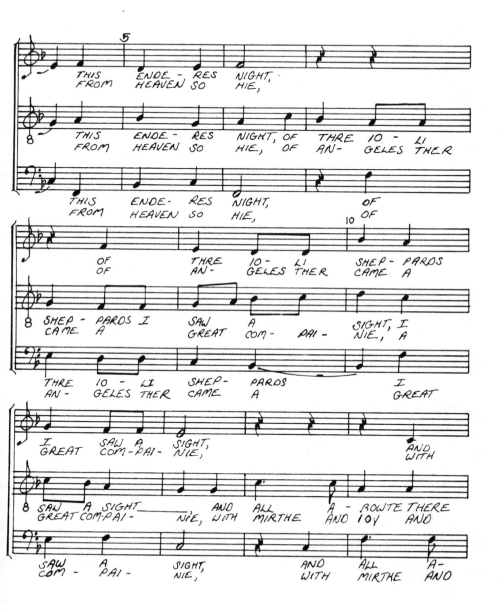

VARIANTS

Bar 3:   Treble, stanza 1, has a semibreve.
Bar 7:   Bass, stanza 2, has two dots instead of a rest.
Bar 8:   Tenor, stanza 2, gives the semibreve as d'; the
           treble semibreve, stanza 2, is omitted.
Bars 10 and 11: The time values of the treble are in excess
           of the other parts. I have, therefore, halved
           the values of the second note, bar 10, and the
           second and third notes, bar 11.
Bar 13:   Tenor, stanza 2, omits the dot after the semibreve.
Bar 14:   Bass, stanza 2, omits the dot after the semibreve.
Bar 15:   Treble, stanza 1, omits the dot after the semibreve.
Bar 16:   Bass, stanza 1, repeats the g semibreve.
Bar 17:   Bass, stanza 1, omits the dot after the semibreve c'.

Bar 18:   Treble, stanza 1, has a' for the first note.
Bar 20:   Tenor, stanza 1, lacks the rest.
           Bass, stanza 2, is a breve; stanza 1 omits the ledger
               line.
           Bass lacks the rest in both stanzas.
Bar 23:   Tenor, stanza 2, gives a semibreve.
Bar 24:   Tenor, stanza 2, lacks the rest and the repetition
               of "They sange terli terlow."
Bar 26:   Treble, stanza 1, lacks the dot.
           Treble, stanza 2, has dots before and after the note,
               and gives a semibreve for the minim.
           Tenor, stanza 1, lacks the second semibreve.
           Bass, stanza 2, gives e for both semibreves.
Bar 29:   Treble, both stanzas, lacks the rest. The second
               stanza ends here, after the two rests.
Bar 33:   Tenor, stanza 2, omits the second minim.
Bar 35:   Bass, stanza 1, omits the breve and following three
               rests.
Bar 39:   The tenor of stanza 2 ends here with the first
               semibreve.
Bar 41:   Bass, stanza 1, has e as the second semibreve.
Bar 42:   Tenor, stanza 1, has g' as the semibreve.

2.   a.   Beholde now hit ys come

     b.   Beholde, now hit ys come to pase,
          That manye yeres before was tolde,
          How that Christ, owre ryght Messyas,
          By Jwdas scholde be bowght and solde!

          For owre offence he man became,
          His fathers wrathe to pacyfye,
          And after, mekely as a lamb,
          Vpon the crose there dyd he dye.

          O Lorde! as thou hast bowght vs all,
          and suffryd at Mownt Callverye,
          Recownfort vs bothe gret and small,
          That yn thy trewth we lyve and dye!

     c.   Coventry, Pageant of the Weavers

     d.   Coventry Corporation MS. A97, The Weavers' Play,
          fol. 17^V

     e.   Hardin Craig, *Two Coventry Corpus Christi Plays*,

2nd ed., EETS, e.s. 87 (1957), 70-71.

Thomas Sharp, *The Presentation in the Temple* (Edinburgh, 1836), p. 86.

3. a. Here is a pottell

    b. Here is a pottell of malmesy, good and stronge,
        it will reioye both hart and tong;
        though noy thinke vs neuer so long
        Yet wee will drinke alyke.

    c. Chester, Noah, p. 57, footnote for line 232

    d. B, fols. 23^v and 24^r
        D, fol. 19^r
        R, fol. 24^v
        W, fol. 19^v
        H, omitted

    e. Deimling and Matthews, *The Chester Plays*, EETS, e.s. 62 (1893; 1959), and 115 (1916; 1959), p. 57.

        Lumiansky and Mills, *The Chester Mystery Cycle*, EETS, s.s. 3 (1974), p. 52.

4. a. Lully, lulla

    b. Lully, lulla, thow littell tine child,
        By by, Lully lullay, thow littell tyne child,
            By by, lully lullay!

        O sisters too,
        How may we do/ For to preserve this day
        This pore yongling/ For whom we do singe
        By by, lully lullay?

        Herod, the king,
        In his raging,/ Chargid he hath this day
        His men of might/ In his owne sight
        All yonge children to slay,

        That wo is me,
        Pore child, for thee,/ And ever morne and may
        For thi parting/ Nether say nor singe,

By by, lully lullay.

c.   Coventry, Pageant of the Shearmen and Taylors

d.   Thomas Sharp, *A Dissertation*, pp. 113-14, 116-17.

e.   *Index of Middle English Verse*, No. 2551.8

Oxford Book of Carols, 1st ed., ed. Percy Dearmer *et al.* (London, 1928), p. 44.

Early English Christmas Carols, ed. Rossell Hope Robbins (New York, 1961), pp. 74-76.

Richard Rastall, *Two Coventry Carols* (Westleigh, Devon: Antico, 1973).

THOMAS SHARP, A DISSERTATION ON THE PAGEANTS ... AT COVENTRY, PP 116-17

VARIANTS

Bar 3:   The bass has "lullaye."
Bar 9:   The bass omits the dot after the first semibreve.
Bar 16:   The treble, stanza 1, has "too" for the breve.
Bar 17:   The treble, stanza 3, has f', semibreve.
           The tenor, stanza 3, has d", breve.
           The bass, stanza 2, has a minim for the semibreve.
Bar 18:   The tenor, stanza 2, omits the rest.
Bar 19:   The treble, stanza 3, has f' for the first semibreve
Bar 20:   The bass, stanza 3, gives c for the second semibreve
Bar 21:   The bass, stanza 1, has "oure" for the semibreve.
Bar 22:   The treble, stanza 2, has b', breve.
           The bass, stanza 3, has d, breve.
Bar 24:   The bass, stanza 3, gives the semibreves as d and c.
Bar 25:   The treble lacks the sharp sign, stanza 1, and the
              rest, stanza 3.
           The tenor lacks the rest in all stanzas; stanza 2
              gives the breve as a semibreve.
           The bass lacks the rest in stanza 2.
Bar 26:   The tenor lacks a sharp sign in all stanzas.
Bar 27:   The treble, stanza 2, gives g' and f' sharp.
Bar 28:   The treble, stanza 2, gives g'.

5.   a.   Rejoyce, rejoyce

     b.   Rejoyce, rejoyce, all that here be!
          The Angell these tythyng[s] hath browght,
          That Simion, before he dye,
          Shalle se the Lorde which all hathe wrowght;

          Wherefore now let vs all prepare
          Owre temple that yn order be!
          For he hathe put awey owre care,
          The Seconde Persone in Trinitye.

     c.   Coventry, Pageant of the Weavers

     d.   Coventry Corporation MS. A97, fol. 17^V

     e.   Hardin Craig, *Two Coventry Corpus Christi Plays*,
          p. 70.

          Thomas Sharp, *The Presentation in the Temple*, p. 86

6.   a.   Save mee o God

b.

c.   Chester, Noah, p. 58, after line 256.

d.   B, fol. 24^r
D, fol. 19^v
H, fol. 16^r
R, fol. 25^r
W, fol. 20^r

7.   a.   Troly loly troly loe

    b.

    c.   Chester, Nativity, p. 151, after line 458.

    d.   B, fol. 57^v
D, fol. 46^v
H, fol. 43^r
R, fol. 62^v
W, fol. 52^v

    e.   Cf. *Index of Middle English Verse*, No. 3800.5

8.   a.   With hart and voyce

    b.   With hart and voyce/ Let us reoiyce
And prayse the Lord alwaye/ For this our joyfull daye,
To se of this our god his majestie,
Who hath given himselfe over us to reygne & to
        governe us.
Lett all our harte reoiyce together,
And lett us all lifte up our voyce, on of us with
        another.

    c.   Norwich, Fall of Man, Play B

    d.   Robert Fitch, "Norwich Pageants. The Grocers'
Play," *Norfolk Archaeology*, 5 (1859), 23.

    e.   Norman Davis, *Non-Cycle Plays and Fragments*, EETS,
s.s. 1 (1970), p. 18.

       Osborn Waterhouse, *The Non-Cycle Mystery Plays*, EETS,
e.s. 104·(1909), p. 18.

Robert Fitch, "Norwich Pageants. The Grocers' Play,"
p. 23.

9. a. Wythe dolorous sorowe

    b. Wythe dolorous sorowe, we maye wayle and wepe
        Both nyght and day in sory sythys full depe.

    c. Norwich, Fall of Man, Play A

    d. Robert Fitch, "Norwich Pageants," p. 15

    e. Norman Davis, *Non-Cycle Plays and Fragments,* p. 11

        Osborn Waterhouse, *The Non-Cycle Mystery Plays,* p.
        11

        Robert Fitch, "Norwich Pageants," p. 15.

III. COMMENTARY ON INDEX OF SONGS

Only nine songs have survived as evidence of the stage
music actually performed in the course of a mystery cycle:
one from Chester, three from York, each set twice, and two
from Coventry. The Chester "Gloria" may be merely a scribal
addition, but the songs from York and Coventry seem to have
been composed especially for the plays of which they are a
part.

British Library MS. Harley 2124, fol. 42^r
    The music for the "Gloria" of the angel in the Chester
Shepherds Play occurs in only this one of the five manuscripts
of the cycle. It is written as part of the text, that is,
centered on the page, in black and white notation.[1]
    The manuscript was copied by three scribes of whom one,
James Miller, apparently supervised the work, and dated it
1607.[2] Miller was a minor canon at Chester Cathedral,[3] but
the identities of the other two scribes are unknown, as are
their connections with Miller and the Cathedral. Scribe A, in
whose hand the music is written, may possibly have added the
song himself, since the shepherds' discussion indicates the
original "Gloria" did not end with "Deo," but included the
words "et in terra pax hominibus."[4] Even if, on the other hand,
he copied it from his exemplar, it may be a unique setting of
the text, for it does not resemble any of the available
medieval musical versions of the "Gloria."[5]

British Library MS. Add. 35,290, fols. 235^V, 236^r, 238^r,
241^r, 241^V
    Six songs belonging to the York Weavers' Play, "The
Appearance of Mary to Thomas," are included in the manuscript
of the cycle.[6] They comprise two settings of each of three
texts, the last of which, however, gives only the incipit and
final word in its second version. The first three settings
occur within the body of the play; the last three are at its
end.
    The six songs bear no likeness to the liturgical settings
of the same texts as they are found in both the York and Sarum
Uses,[7] and, hence, were probably composed especially for the
play. The first three are written in score, the last three in

separate parts; the scribe has used black and red notation.
The technique of gymel--two-part polyphony based on thirds,
sixths, and tenths--is here characterized by crossing voices,
and with the basically note-against-note style, it points to
an English composer of these songs. John Stevens suggests, on
the basis of style and notation, a mid-fifteenth-century date
for the music; this is close to the first estimates of
1430-40 as the date for the manuscript. The most recent
dating of the manuscript, however, has favored a time around
1475,[8] but the music could still belong, of course, to the
earlier period.

The songs are not stylistically dissimilar to other
fifteenth-century English vocal music, and incorporate many
of the characteristics of the conductus and the carol. The
score notation, single text, and original tenor of the conductus are found in these York pieces; the rhythmic oddities,
gymel, lack of imitation, and the coincidence of musical and
textual phrasing are seen also in carols of this period.[9]

Relationships exist between the first and second settings
of each text. "Surge" II is a free elaboration of the shorter
version; in both, each phrase (except "propera mea") opens
and closes with the same notes, but the development of the
phrases is more florid in the second setting. The phrases
"vasculum vite" are almost exactly the same in both; "Surge"
II adds only an ornamental figure to one note.

In "Veni de libano," special emphasis is placed on the
second occurrence of the word "veni" in both versions by means
of long note values. In addition, the two songs have similar
descending figures in the treble for "coronaberis."

The settings of "Veni electa," however, are less dependent
on one another. Only the openings of the songs, in their
choices of pitches and melismatic style in which a group of
notes is sung to one syllable, are similar.

That two versions of each song should have been given is
surprising. Perhaps the capabilities of the singers determined
the choice, or perhaps the requirements of a particular year's
performance decided which setting was to be used.

Thomas Sharp, A Dissertation of the Pageants . . . at Coventry,
pp. 115-17

The two songs from the Coventry Shearmen and Taylors' Play
were added in 1591 to the 1534 manuscript of the play. The
scribe was, presumably, Thomas Mawdycke.[10]

Both settings of the carol texts appear to be original,[11]
but R. L. Greene suggests that the melody of "Lully" may be
common to other lullaby carols;[12] no other use of this melody,
however, has yet been located.

The songs are in three generally homorhythmic parts.
"As I out rode" has points of imitation in the burden section, and tenor and bass parts show voice exchange in the
phrase "They sange terli terlow." Greene feels that the
setting tends to obscure the carol-with-burden form, but a
free style is not uncommon in other sixteenth-century
English carols.[13] The rhythm in "Lully" shifts from duple
to triple meter at the beginning, and back to duple for one
bar at authentic cadences (bars 7, 12, 22, 27); modern
editors have coped with this by lengthening time values
and adding rests.[14] A *signum congruentiae* ﹖S﹒ occurs
under four notes in the treble and bass parts.[15] Although
it seems to act as a warning that the note progression will
change in the following stanza, the changes to which it
points are not harmonically correct and cannot have been
intended. Such a use of the *signum* is not customary; John
Stevens, in *Music at the Court of Henry VIII*, notes a similar sign in his sources, and takes it to indicate, in
various contexts, a repetition, canonic entrance, *da Capo*
sign specifying that the section is to be repeated from the
beginning, *dal Segno* directing that the section is to be
repeated from the place where the sign is located, pause,
or *ouvertclos* sign. He cautions, however, that the "exact
meaning is not always clear."[16]

The music as printed by Sharp purports to be an exact
copy, in black and white notation and separate parts, of
the manuscript. The variants among stanzas are so numerous
and so musically incorrect, however, that one must question
the accuracy of either the original scribes or of Sharp's
transliteration.

Although only the nine songs just discussed occur in
the cycles with both words and music, a total of fifty-five
different Latin songs, indicated by their incipits, in
addition to thirty-four unnamed songs, indicated by stage
directions, occur in the texts of the extant mystery plays.
All but fourteen of the identifiable songs can be located
in the English liturgical Uses.[17]

Both the Proper and Ordinary of the Mass and all sung
parts of the Office provide the sources of the texts named
in the plays; the antiphons of the Office are, however, the
most frequently drawn from. The possible source-melodies
supply even more choice. For example, the liturgical tunes
can vary for the same text: "Venite benedicti" occurs as
two different liturgical types--an antiphon and an introit--
and the music for each is different.[18] Distinctions in the
rank of feasts also influence the ritual music: "Exultet

celum," a hymn, has five melodies, depending on its location
in the liturgy.[19] The liturgical customs of English monastic
and secular churches provide still additional choice:
"Salvator mundi" is sung to the melody of "Veni creator" in
secular uses.[20] Finally, "Stella coeli," an antiphon sung
in times of plague, had no standard plainsong as a setting.[21]

This is not to say, of course, that because the texts
are liturgical, the melodies used in the plays must be so as
well; any text could have had a new setting. Indeed, "Veni
electa mea," from the York Weavers' Play, and the Chester
"Gloria" are such instances.[22] They are, unfortunately, the
only surviving compositions used as stage music in the mystery plays to combine liturgical texts with non-liturgical
music.

Many of the songs are taken from the liturgy of the
feasts celebrating the same action as that which the plays
retell. "Accipite spiritum," an antiphon from Lauds of
Pentecost, occurs in the Chester Sending of the Holy Spirit;
"Ascendo ad patrem" from the Chester, Towneley, and York
Ascension plays is from Lauds of Ascension Day. A partic-
ularly apt congruence occurs with "Alma chorus," a sequence
sung in the *Ludus Coventriae* Betrothal of Mary; the editors
of the *Analecta Hymnica* note that it was often used in
England for the Nuptial Mass.[23] "Gloria laus" from the
Ludus Coventriae entry into Jerusalem was sung during the
Palm Sunday procession. Choir boys located "*in eminentiori
loco*" sang first the refrain, "Gloria laus," answered by the
choir in the procession, then the verses, each of which was
followed by the refrain sung by those below.[24] The play
attempts to reproduce this ceremony by having Christ met by
"chylderyn with flowrys . . . and they synggyn Gloria
laus. . . ."

Other exact correspondences are "Assumpta es[t] Maria"
(the *Ludus Coventriae* Assumption), both an antiphon and an
alleluia verse for the feast of the Assumption; "Christus
resurgens" (Chester, Towneley, and York Resurrection plays),
an antiphon before Matins on Easter morning; "De terra,"
sung while the Apostles in the *Ludus Coventriae* Assumption
bury the body of the Virgin Mary, and taken from the ceremony
of the inhumation of the dead; and "Exiit Israel," a psalm
in the burial service, sung in the same play during the
procession to Mary's tomb.[25]

Liturgical dramas, as forerunners and also contemporaries of mystery cycles, could have been sources of songs
associated with particular dramatic situations common to
both types of plays.[26] Some songs do, in fact, appear in
both, but certainty as to borrowing is impossible for several

reasons: English manuscripts containing liturgical plays are rare, and although continental usage probably prevailed, one simply cannot be sure; the liturgy is a common background for both; correspondences could be due more to aptness of the texts than to borrowing. The following are songs common to liturgical and vernacular plays; those from the Latin drama are contained in continental manuscripts, and may, or may not, represent similar English practices.

"Ascendo ad patrem" and "Christus resurgens," both in the Chester, Towneley, and York Ascension and Resurrection plays, also occur in *Visitatio* dramas; "Gloria in excelsis," as one would expect, is found in many Christmas plays; "Gloria laus," the hymn for the *Ludus Coventriae* Entry into Jerusalem, appears in the Passion Play contained in the *Carmina Burana* manuscript; the "Magnificat" and "Ne timeas Maria" from Chester and York are sung in fourteenth-century Italian plays; "Veni creator" is included in the Avignon Presentation of the late fourteenth century; "Gloria tibi Trinitas" and "Venite benedicti," both from the Chester cycle, occur in late fifteenth-century German Passion Plays; and the "Te Deum" is the conclusion not only of many liturgical plays, but also of Matins, its ritual setting.[27]

Even with the addition to the foregoing songs of "Accipite spiritum," "Assumpta es[t]," "Nunc dimittis," and "Viri Galilei,"[28] which occur in dramatic ceremonies, not plays, performed on the feasts of Pentecost, the Assumption, the Purification, and the Ascension, the hypothesis that familiarity with a song occasioned its borrowing is not necessarily substantiated, since the liturgical association is, in each instance, equally strong.

The Chester Ascension is, however, a special problem. Three of the songs in the antiphonal section sung between Christ and the angels, "Quis est iste," "Iste formosus," and "Torculor [sic] calcavi," occur in the Fleury *Peregrinus* play,[29] but none of the five appears in any medieval liturgy of which I am aware.[30] They are, on the other hand, antiphons for the modern feast of the Precious Blood, but the melodies given in the *Liber Usualis* are quite different from those in the Fleury play.[31] Medieval offices for the feast of the Precious Blood as celebrated in cities having relics and hence a special devotion to it also reveal no similarities to the modern texts,[32] and attempts to find contemporary dramatic analogues using the same source, *Isaiah* 63.1-3, have proved fruitless. The *Passion de Semur*[33] does not contain the incident, and Arnoul Greban's *Passion*, although including the Ascension and reception to heaven, does not have the antiphons.[34] The *Stanzaic Life of Christ*, a fourteenth-century non-dramatic work incorporating the episode, quotes these lines from *Isaiah* as prophecies,[35] but only at Chester are they dramatized and specified as sung to what are, presumably, free compositions.

The Chester author frequently provides songs not found elsewhere. The angel in the Slaughter of the Innocents sings "Ecce Dominus" as the Holy Family flees to Egypt. This song occurs neither in the liturgy nor in other plays containing the same incident, such as Greban's *Passion* or the *Carmina Burana* liturgical play of the "King of Egypt."[36] The *Stanzaic Life of Christ* quotes the text as an interline,[37] and the ultimate source is *Isaiah* 19.1, but Chester is alone in choosing a relevant text to be sung to a melody that is probably original.

The most striking example of the Chester playwright's originality is the song "Hec est ara Dei coeli," sung in the Nativity play by the angel as Octavian sees the vision of the Virgin and Child. Although French plays contain the incident, the phrase is spoken, not sung, and with somewhat different words. In *Le Mystère du vieil testament*, Octavian claims he has heard the voice from heaven say, "Vecy l'autel du Filz de Dieu . . . ," while in the "Grand Passion" of the Valenciennes manuscript, he declares he wishes an altar built and "Qu'i soit nommé Ara cely." In *Le Mystère de l'Incarnation et Nativité*, the angel Uriel announces to Octavian and the Sibyl regarding the vision that "Il est nommé Autel du ciel/ Ainsi appeller tu le dois."[38] Two non-dramatic analogues, the thirteenth-century *Legenda Aurea* of Jacobus of Voragine and the *Stanzaic Life of Christ*, give the same text as Chester, but their angels merely say the words and do not sing them.[39]

How the song is performed is indicated by the direction "fiat nota secundum arbitrium agentis, etc.," an unusual rubric that signifies less that the actor may sing whatever he chooses, perhaps, than that he is to use judgment in the manner of his singing.[40] A more practical consideration may be in evidence here as well: the song accompanies Octavian's ritual offering of incense and would have to last as long as the actual procedure of incensing; the direction would then instruct the singer to suit his improvization to the stage action. That these Chester songs not found in the liturgy are probably original compositions seems clear; they are, as well, examples of independent and creative use of non-dramatic sources.

A complete group of texts taken from non-dramatic sources and used as songs are those in the *Ludus Coventriae* Assumption, two of which occur with original music in the York cycle.

The eight songs forming Mary's dirge are chanted by Christ,
the Apostles, and Mary, and accompany her reception into
heaven by the angels and martyrs. The source of these texts
is essentially the *Legenda Aurea* where they occur in exactly
the same situation and order,[41] but some are also found in
the liturgy.

"Veni tu electa mea," the first song of the section,
differs not only from the version in the *Legenda Aurea* but
also from that in the York Appearance of Our Lady to Thomas
in its insertion of "tu"; both York and the *Ludus Coventriae*
have "quia concupivit rex speciem tuam," while the *Legenda
Aurea* gives "concupivi" and omits "rex." The text given in
the York play appears as a respond and an alleluia verse in
the York and Sarum uses, with York using it again as an
antiphon.[42]

A respond provides the text of "Paratum cor meum"; in
the *Legenda Aurea*, however, the song is "Paratum cor meum,
domine [*Ludus Coventriae*, "deus"], paratum cor meum," while
Ludus Coventriae adds, as does the liturgical form, "cantabo
et psalmum dicam domino." In the play, "Hec est que nescivit
thorum in delictis/ habebit requiem in respectu animarum
sanctarum" varies from both the liturgy and the *Legenda Aurea*
by substituting "requiem," rather more suitable for the dirge
being sung, for "fructum," and, as a result, replacing "in
refectione" of the sources with "in respectu." "Beatam me
dicent" is the same in all three versions, but the text of
the song which follows it, "Veni de libano," occurring in
York as well, varies in the *Ludus Coventriae* play. Both
the York song and the *Legenda Aurea* omit "mea"; the liturgy
provides two only approximate sources: "Veni a libano
sponsa, veni a libano" from the antiphon "Ibo mihi," and
"Veni de libano, veni coronaberis," which is the conclusion
of the antiphon "Tota pulchra es."[43] Scriptural echoes seem
also to be present: the *Song of Songs* 4.8 has "Veni de
libano, sponsa mea, veni de libano, veni coronaberis."

The next three songs are identical with the *Legenda Aurea*
texts, and parts also appear in the liturgy: the last
section of "Ecce venio," "exultavit spiritus meus in deo
salutari meo," the first section of "Que est ista que
assendit de deserto deliciis affluens . . . ," and the first
section of "Ista est speciosa inter filias Jerusalem sicut
vidistis eam plenam caritate et dilectione. . . ."[44]

Although two other texts, "Virgo prudentissima" and
"Surge proxima," remain in this section in the *Legenda Aurea*,
the *Ludus Coventriae* play includes only the second, translated into English and spoken by Christ as Mary's body is
assumed into heaven.[45] "Surge proxima mea, columba mea,

tabernaculum glorie, vasculum vite, templum celeste," the
first passage of the text, occurs in the York cycle as well,
where it is set to music twice.[46] The York scribe was,
perhaps, more familiar with the liturgical and scriptural
analogues than with the *Legenda Aurea* source, for in the
second setting he has written, "Surge propera mea," which is
the word the *Song of Songs* 2.10 and the antiphon "Tota pulchra
es" both use in this phrase.[47]

The playwright of the *Ludus Coventriae* has made creative
use of his sources, the liturgy, scripture, and the *Legenda
Aurea*. He selects and adapts texts, varying as he sees fit
their words and even their presentation to suit his concept
of the play. The significance is evident: by supplementing
his non-dramatic source with the liturgy and by having the
entire scene sung, the dramatist has gone beyond the notion
of mere "incidental" music. The scene's dialogue in music
between Christ and Mary, commented on by the chorus of
Apostles and concluded by a summing-up question and reply by
choruses of martyrs and angels, is an original treatment of
source material to achieve a decidedly dramatic effect.

A choice based on the appropriateness of the text can
be made between the two possible songs indicated by the incipit "Dignus es domine" in the Chester Fall of Lucifer. The
antiphon "Dignus es domine deus noster, accipere gloriam et
honorem et virtutem; quia tu creasti omnia, et propter
voluntatem tuam erant et creata sunt: salus Deo nostro qui
sedet super thronum et Agno. Alleluia," is more suitable
to the action of the creation of the angels than is the
respond "Dignus es domine, accipere librum et aperire sig-
nacula ejus: quoniam occisus es et redemisti nos Deo, in
sanguine tuo. Alleluia." Although the incipits differ in
the five manuscripts, with H and D omitting it completely,
R giving "Dignus dei," W directing "Dignus es dei," and only
B supplying "Dignus es domine," a certain measure of cor-
roboration for B's version is afforded by the marginal note
in D, "forsan pro agnus," which recalls the text of the
antiphon.[48]

The *Ludus Coventriae* cycle has two sung items that are
not definitely traceable. The blessing given by Ysakar in
the Conception of Mary is preceded by a common formula sung
here by the Chorus and one of the Ministers, but the precise
words of the actual benediction do not occur in Sarum or
York manuals.[49]

In the same cycle's Temptation of Christ, angels sing
"Gloria tibi Domine," which is the incipit of the last stanza,
the doxology, in a number of Office hymns. It is also a
response to the announcement of the Gospel reading at Masses

and Baptisms, but the direction does not indicate which text is to be sung.[50]

"Laus tibi cum gloria," which concludes the York Harrowing of Hell, is another text I have been unable to locate. It may be an error for the Trinity Sunday verse, "Tibi laus, tibi gloria,/ Tibi gratiarum actio."[51]

Finally, the Towneley cycle has one song with no apparent source. In the Thomas of India play, Christ suddenly appears "et cantat pax vobis et non tardabit."[52] He sings again, eight lines later, in a second sudden appearance. The text of the song is not found in the liturgy, nor in any liturgical play; the subject of the appearance of Christ to the disciples after the Resurrection occurs in the other cycles, but only in Towneley is there a song. Chester and York give Christ's words in this scene as: "Pees vnto yowe euermore myght be,/ Drede you noȝt, for I am hee . . . ," and "Peace amongst you, Brethren fayre!/ yea, dread you not, in no maner. . . ." Towneley itself has, for Christ's first spoken words, "Peasse amangys you euer ichon!/ it is I, drede you noght. . . ."[53] It should be noted, too, that the text "Pax vobis et nolite timere" occurs as an antiphon at Vespers on the modern feast of St. Gabriel, although I cannot locate it in a medieval source. I suspect, therefore, that the Towneley "Pax vobis" refers to the song "Pax vobis et nolite timere," and that "et non tardabit" with which the stage direction ends is not part of the song's text, but is a direction for an immediate exit to the actor playing Christ, and is repeated in the second occurrence through a scribal error. That the stage direction is repeated because Christ makes yet another brief appearance before he finally visits Thomas is, of course, possible. "Pax vobis" is sung three times in liturgical plays on the subject.[54]

Of the thirty-three songs requiring a choral performance in the plays, only three are definitely polyphonic. The three York songs, written for two voices in all six settings, are sung by twelve angels. The York "Ave regina celorum," from the Death of Mary play, may be a fourth polyphonic song. It is sung by the four angels whose speeches conclude the action, along with a devil ("uno diabolo"), whose presence in the play is accounted for by Christ's words "But modir, þe fende muste be nedis at þyne endyng,/ In figoure full foule for to fere þe." Why the devil, rather than any of the other characters, should be one of the singers is puzzling, but the direction is clear. Symbolism through music may be intended here, however: in being assumed both body and soul into heaven, Mary conquers death and its progenitor, the devil; she is queen not only of heaven, then, but also of hell.[55] "Ave regina" is also sung in the *Ludus Coventriae* Visitation by a chorus, but no other indications of its performance are given by the actor who, as Contemplacio, concludes the play, "Ave regina celorum · to oure lady we synge."[56]

Seven songs, the number of whose singers can be inferred from the persons in the cast and the stage directions, could be performed as solo polyphony: "Accipite spiritum," "Ascendo ad patrem," "Christus resurgens," "Laetamini," "Simeon justus," and "Veni creator" are performed by two angels; "Stella coeli" is sung by three shepherds. "Exaltare," "Viri Galilei," and "Cantemus domino" use four singers, and could be sung as either solo or choral polyphony.[57] The other songs employ choirs ranging from seven to twelve singers, and hence could be sung in choral polyphony, as could those where, titles or incipits of songs not included in the stage directions, the context provides the number of singers.[58] Whether polyphony might have been used in many of the choral performances of the Ludus Coventriae cycle cannot be surmised, for the majority of both the heavenly and earthly choirs seem to be composed of indeterminate numbers of non-acting singers.[59]

This heavenly music, always liturgical and usually sung by angels who do not have speaking roles, is concentrated in the plays dealing with the life and death of the Virgin. Of the forty-one pieces in the entire cycle, twenty-seven occur in the Mary plays. Of these, twenty-one are performed by choirs, twelve of which are angelic. Few plays in the other cycles use angelic choirs: only the Chester Creation and the York Creation, Appearance of Our Lady, and the Assumption include them. Moreover, only in the York Appearance of Our Lady are there what could be considered to be the non-acting angels who are so frequent in the *Ludus Coventriae* and who would have been excessively costly for an ordinary craft guild to include in its production.[60] The number of angelic songs in the Mary plays and the non-acting function of the singers seem to support the view that these plays were conceived separately from the others in the cycle, and lead one to suspect the possibility that they were sponsored, if not acted, by some clerical or semi-religious group which had the skill, training, and members to perform songs taken not from the everyday liturgy but from that used on special occasions.[61]

The use of the same song in plays on the same subject but in different cycles shows some variety. "Ascendo" is sung in the Towneley and York Ascension plays by angels, but in Chester by Christ; the latter performance is obviously more suitable to the text. "Christus resurgens," sung by angels in the Towneley and Chester plays, is performed as a solo by one angel in the York Resurrection, even though the

play is substantially the same in this section as the Towneley
version. "Hosanna filio David" is sung by the crowd welcoming
Christ in both the York and Chester Entry into Jerusalem plays;
the singers are boys alone at York, for one of the Burgesses
says, "With myghtfull songes her on a rawe,/ Our childir
schall/ Go synge before. . . ." At Chester, the boys are
joined by the citizens: "Tunc ibunt pueri versus Ierusalem
cum ramis palmarum in manibus; et Cives prosternent vestimenta
sua in via, et cantabunt 'hosanna. . .'."[62]

Songs are usually correctly assigned to the characters
who ought to sing them: Mary, for example, sings the "Magnificat" in the Chester and York Visitation plays, but the
canticle "Nunc dimittis" is sung by Simeon only in the Chester
Purification. The *Ludus Coventriae* has an ambiguous stage
direction: "Nunc dimittis seruum tuum domine,' etcetera.
The psalme songyn every vers and þer qwyl Symeon pleyth with
þe child. . . ." Does Simeon sing while he plays with the
child, or is a choir of non-acting singers involved in the
play? The only other characters named are Anna, Joseph, Mary,
and the priest, none of whom, logically, should sing the
canticle. In the *Ludus Coventriae* Assumption "Veni electa
mea" and "Veni de libano" are sung, fittingly, by Christ to
Mary, but in the York Appearance of Our Lady they are performed by the twelve angels who accompany Mary to heaven.

Two songs occur in plays similar in theme if not in subject. The angels in the Chester Last Judgment have the
choice of singing either "Laetamini in Domino" or "Salvator
mundi"; Towneley's saved souls in the Harrowing of Hell are
given the latter song, but only the first verse. Finally,
the "Te Deum" is sung by choruses in all the plays in which
it occurs: angels in the York Creation, the saved souls in
the Chester and Towneley Harrowings and in the Towneley
Judgment.

The extant English songs from the cycles consist of two
with words and music, five with texts only, two incipits, and
a number of tags which may or may not be from contemporary
songs.

The two plays from Coventry provide "As I out rode this
enderes night" and "Lully, lulla," the famous Coventry Carol,
as well as the texts for two more songs.[63] As the end of the
Shearmen and Taylors' Nativity Pageant, Thomas Sharp prints,
from his transcription of the play, the inscription, "Theise
songes/ belonge to/ The Taylors & Shearemens Pagant./ The
firste and the laste the Sheapheards singe/ And the Second or
Middlemost the Women Singe./ Thomas Mawdycke." Mawdycke,
presumably the original scribe, gives the date as May 13, 1591.

Of course, the "firste and the laste" songs are actually the two stanzas of "As I out rode," not different pieces.[64]

R. L. Greene, in his *Early English Carols*, notes two possible analogues for "As I out rode": in Bodleian MS. Eng. poet. e. I, "Tyrle tyrlo," which he dates after 1450, and Balliol College MS. 354, "Tyrly, tirlow," which he suggests dates from before 1536.[65] The Coventry song appears to be a version of the first two stanzas of the Bodleian carol:

> Tyrle, tyrlo,
> So merylye the shepperdes began to blowe.
> Abowt the fyld thei pyped full right,
> Even abowt the middes off the nyght;
> Adown frome heven thei saw cum a lyght.
> Tyrle, tirlo.
>
> Off angels ther came a company
> With mery songes and melody;
> The shepperdes annone gane them aspy.
> Tyrle, tyrlo.

The Balliol text has, for the last line of the first stanza, "Adown from heven that ys so hygh," a variant closer to the Coventry words.[66] "Lully" is thought by Greene to be an original carol written specifically for the play in which it occurs. He suggests that the melody, on the other hand, was borrowed, but gives no evidence for this supposition.[67]

The manuscript of the Weavers' Pageant still exists, and in it, the texts for two of its songs.[68] Thomas Mawdycke would appear to have been the scribe who once again added the songs to the copy of the play, but no date is given. The first, "Rejoyce, rejoyce," is suitable for inclusion in the play as it has obvious reference to the theme of the Presentation of Jesus in the Temple; the first two lines of the second stanza, "Wherefore now let vs all prepare/ Owre temple that in order be," indicate it is the first song of the play, performed by Simeon and his clerks as they go "vp to the tempull."[69] The second song, "Beholde now hit ys come to pase," is, however, in its celebration of the Redemption unsuited to the action of both the Presentation and the Finding of Christ in the Temple; there is no relevant place for its performance, although four directions for singing are given in the play.[70] At the end of the song is written the name of James Hewett who, as noted above, was a wait in the employ of Coventry Corporation. His musical career in Coventry as I have been able to trace it began in 1554 with his being paid for playing the regals in the Weavers' Pageant. The first recorded payment to him by the Corporation was in 1562, the last in 1584. In 1563, he was hired by the Drapers to play the regals for their pageant. Since his occupation was that of musician, it seems likely he could have composed as well as performed the music.[71]

Two of Hewett's fellow-waits were Richard Saddler and Richard Stiff, both receiving waits' fees from the Chamberlains in 1566. Stiff's name occurs irregularly from this year in payments of waits' wages; in 1590 the Wardens paid twenty shillings "to old Stiffe Late one of the waites. . . ."[72] The name "Rychard" is written at the end of the first Weavers' song, and it is possible that one of the waits of that name was the composer of "Rejoyce, rejoyce." Thomas Nicolls, a wait in 1566, set songs for the Drapers in that year and for the Cappers in 1569,[73] and even though the Weavers' accounts do not itemize a like payment, their general expenditures for music might well have included fees to the waits James Hewett and "Richard" for similar services.

Both versions of the Norwich Grocers' Play contain texts of songs. The song that concludes the 1565 production is headed "Old Musick Triplex Tenor Medius Bass." The text of the song then follows.[74]

The description of the musical setting of the earlier 1533 song is more revealing, however: "These last 2 lines set to musick twice over and again for a Chorus of 4 pts."[75] If this summary statement can be interpreted to mean that the song "Wythe dolorous sorowe we maye wayle and wepe both nyght & day in sory sythys full depe" was set as a solo, first for Adam, then for Eve, and last, as a four-part chorus, what was sung may have been akin to the verse anthem. Peter Le Huray, in *Music and the Reformation*, notes that an antiphonal performance with instrumental obbligato provided a simple type of verse anthem, and that the repetition of the text could be made by a chorus.[76] The Norwich song appears to possess these characteristics, and, in addition, has the necessary accompaniment in the "organs" used in this particular performance.[77]

The composer of the song was probably Stephen Prewett who was paid by the Grocers "for makyng of a newe ballet."[78] Prewett was a parish priest in Norwich from at least 1536; one wonders if he could be the "Dominus Stephanus prowet" who composed two antiphons of which only two voices of each remain in two early sixteenth-century manuscripts.[79]

Only the 1607 manuscript of the Chester play contains the incipit of the song of Noah and his family, "Save mee o God," although the other four manuscripts do indicate singing at this point.[80] Of the two psalms, 54 and 69, that begin with these words, Psalm 69.1-2 is obviously more apt:

> Save me O god: for the waters are come in,
> even unto my soul. I stick fast in the deep
> mire, where no ground is. I am come into
> deep waters, so that the floods run over me.[81]

The possible styles of performance are numerous: the
psalm could be sung as prose in a modified Sarum chant, or
in "English" chant as found in Merbecke's *Book of Common
Prayer Noted*,[82] or as a free polyphonic composition. Although Sternhold and Hopkins' metrical psalter set mono-
phonically appeared in 1556, the earliest printed setting of
Psalm 69 in this form did not appear until 1561:

> Save me, O God, and that with speed,
>   the waters flow full fast
> So nigh my soul do they proceed
>   that I am sore aghast
> I stick full deep in filth and clay,
>   whereas I feel no ground
> I fall into such floods, I say,
>   that I am like be drown'd. . . .[83]

Part settings of the metrical text began appearing from
1563.[84] Thus, Noah and his family could have sung either a
prose or a metrical psalm, in monophony or in polyphony, in
a traditional setting, or in an original composition.

A second song in the same play is called such in only
one manuscript: W, the second earliest, copied in 1592 by
George Bellin, a professional scribe.[85] A section of twelve
lines in W is headed "The Good Gossippes Songe"; R, the copy
written by Bellin in 1600, has "The good Gossipes," as do
D (1591, the earliest manuscript) and B (1604). H (1607)
merely gives "Gossip," and omits the last four lines.[86] The
text is:

> The flood comes in, full fleetinge fast,
> on every side it spredeth full fare;
> for feare of drowning I am agast,
> good gossip, let us draw neare.
>
> And let vs drinke or we depart,
> for often tymes we have done soe;
> for at a draught thou drinkes a quarte,
> and so will I doe or I goe.

here is a pottell of malmesy, good and stronge,
It will reioye both hart and tong;
though noy thinke vs neuer so long
yet wee will drinke alyke.

The first eight lines are an obvious insertion, for their
versification is in cross rhyme, while the rest of the pageant
is in *rime couée*.[87]
One suspects that these eight lines are a revision of
older material of which only the four lines beginning "Here
is a pottell" remain; perhaps the reviser thought the original
unsuited to the morally-elevated action of the play. The
scribe of H, a century later, may have omitted the whole
"pottell of malmesy" stanza for similar reasons. Such evidence of the scribe's sense of propriety tends to establish
at least an occupational connection between him and James
Miller, the supervisor of the copying and a minor canon at
Chester Cathedral.[88]
A second possible example of his exercising a discrim-
inatory hand occurs in the Shepherds play, where all manuscripts but H direct the shepherds to "singe troly loly
troly loe." The scribe of H has, on the other hand, "Tunc
omnes pastores cum aliis adiuvantibus cantabunt hilare
carmen."[89] His reference to the others helping the shepherds
to sing is intriguing, since the only additional characters
in this manuscript's version of the play are Joseph, Mary, and
the angel, none of whom should logically join in the song. The
other four manuscripts, however, have four boys presenting
gifts to the Christ Child;[90] that these may be meant as the
extra singers is substantiated by the accounts of the producing
guild, the Painters: their accounts regularly include payments
for "sheperds' boys" who seem to be choirboys from the
Cathedral.[91] The song they all sing is obviously in the vernacular with "Troly loly" as its refrain, a common use for
the phrase. John Stevens gives three examples of this refrain in his *Music at the Court of Henry VIII*: a three-part
song by Cornish and two anonymous pieces.[92] Joseph Ritson
considers the refrain to be "of great antiquity," noting its
occurrence in, among other works, *Piers Plowman* and Skelton's
Comely Coistrown. Nan Cooke Carpenter points out its
appearance as a tag in *Hickscorner*.[93]
Other words and phrases that could be drawn from vernacular songs are scattered through the cycles. The *Ludus
Coventriae* Trial of Joseph and Mary makes reference to a
lullaby, with "ffayr chylde lullay sone must she syng," as
does the Towneley Second Shepherds' play, "Syng lullay thou
shall."[94] The two prophets in the Coventry Shearmen and

Taylors' play discuss the birth of Christ and the shepherds'
visit to Bethlehem; they conclude:

> He reywardid them full well:
> He graunt them hevyn ther-in to dwell;
>   In ar the gon with joie and myrthe,
> And there songe hit ys "neowell."[95]

Numerous epithets of grief and sorrow occur. Mary mourns over
Christ with "Alas! may euer be my sang" and "Sore syghyng is
my sang" in the Towneley Crucifixion.[96] In York and Towneley,
God promises that Pharoah's "song shall be 'alas'," while
Ffroward, in the Towneley Buffeting, bitterly comments, "I
may syng ylla-hayll." Distress is commonly expressed by "my
song may be well awaye!"[97]

How many of the directions for singing refer to vernacular songs is impossible to determine, but if one can presume
on the basis of "As I out rode" and "Troly loly" that the
shepherds' songs for which no incipits are given would also
have been in English, a tentative suggestion regarding their
performance can be made. The Towneley, York, and Chester
Shepherds plays all have three shepherds who sing three songs
which are probably like the Chester "Troly loly."[98] Only in
Towneley, however, is the style of singing described. In
the Second Shepherds' play, the three shepherds decide that
a song would help pass the long night:

> Primus pastor. lett me syng the tenory.
> ij us pastor. And I the tryble so hye.
> iij us pastor. Then the meyne fallys to me;
>   lett se how ye chauntt.[99]

At the end of the First Shepherds' play, they leave Bethlehem
praising Christ:

> . . . To the lawde of this lam
> Syng we in syght.[100]

On the basis of these two passages, Nan Cooke Carpenter pos-
tulates their singing to be in discant style, in which there
is a "given tenor, [and] parallel countermelodies (improvised
at sight) in the treble and mean."[101]

If, indeed, the melody upon which the shepherds discant,
the *cantus firmus*, is in the tenor, what they are singing
could be the so-called "Freemen's Songs" (perhaps a corruption
of "Three-men's Songs"). These pieces, some of which were
composed by Cornish and, it is thought, Henry VIII, were

exceedingly popular,[102] as a London court prohibition of
1553 indicates: everyone, whether freeman or not, is pro-
hibited from singing "any songs commonly called three men's
songs . . . in or at any tavern, inn, alehouse, weddings,
feasts, or any other like place . . . (except the same be
sung in a common play or interlude)" because such singing is
to the "great loss, prejudice and hindrance" of the minstrels' company.[103] They are mentioned in the *Castle of
Perseverance* in the context of much the same sort of con-
viviality:

> Thyrti thousende þat I wel knowe
> In my lyf louely I lede
>   þat had leuere syttyn at þe ale
> Thre mens songys to syngyn lowde
> Þanne toward þe chyrche for to crowde.[104]

Thus, their contemporary connections make them not unlikely
songs for shepherds to sing, and perhaps a freeman's song, by
its nature and associations, was in the mind of the Chester
scribe when he specified that his shepherds were to sing
"hilare carmen."

IV. INDEX OF INSTRUMENTS MENTIONED IN THE CYCLES AND ACCOUNTS

BEAM
A long metal horn or trumpet which tapers from a small
mouthpiece to an open end with an expanding bell. It was
used for battle or hunting signals.

Chester	Fall of Lucifer	p. 18, line 228	B, fol. 6^r
			D, missing
			H, fol. 3^v
			R, fol. 7^v
			W, fol. 4^r
Chester	Judgment	p. 428, line 33;	B, fol. 166^v
		p. 429, line 46	D, fol. 142^v
			H, fol. 131^v
			R, fol. 194^v
			W, fol. 162^r
Towneley	Prophets	p. 62, line 199	T, fol. 19^v
York	Judgment	p. 499, lines 63 and 65	Y, fol. 246^v

BELLS
Probably chime bells: from four to nine bells suspended in
a frame or on a stand and played with one or two hammers.

Coventry	Weavers	p. 45, line 366	C, fol. 5^v
		p. 52, line 624	C, fol. 9^r
		p. 53, line 633	C, fol. 9^r
Towneley	Purification	p. 184, line 104	T, fol. 61^v
		p. 185, line 114	

CITHARA
A triangular or quadrilateral harp with from eight to
eighteen strings tuned diatonically.

| *Ludus Coventriae* | Assumption | p. 358, after line 90 | LC, fol. 216^r |

CORNU
The word used in the Chester stage direction to translate
"horn." See below.

Chester	Shepherds	p. 134, after line 48	B, omitted, fol. 51^v
			D, fol. 42^r
			H, fol. 38^v
			R, fol. 55^v
			W, fol. 46^v

FLUTE
Although this could be a transverse flute or a recorder, the
context suggests it is the common three-hole flute, or
"tabor pipe."

| Chester | Late Banns | p. 6, line 118 | B, fol. 1^v |
| | | | R, fol. 2^v |

HARP
See "CITHARA" above.

Chester	Late Banns, crossed out	p. 6, line 118	B, fol. 1^v
			R, fol. 2^v
Towneley	Prophets	p. 60, line 110	T, fol. 19^r

HORN
An uncurved instrument of conical bore, most frequently
made of hollowed wood or horn and bound with metal bands.
It was used by herdsmen for signals, and may have been the
medieval "trumpe."

Chester	Shepherds	p. 138, line 159; p. 139, lines 163, 168, 169, 172	B, fol. 53^r
			D, fol. 43^r and 43^v
			H, fol. 39^v and 40^r
			R, fol. 57^v
			W, fol. 48^r
Towneley	Judgment	p. 367, line 3	T, fol. 122^r
		p. 368, line 42	T, fol. 122^r
		p. 370, line 89	T, fol. 123^r
		p. 375, line 250	T, fol. 124^v
York	Judgment	p. 500, line 115	Y, fol. 247^v

ORGAN
    A keyboard instrument with wind supplied to the pipes by
    bellows; either the small portatives (slung over the
    player's shoulder) or positives (moveable, but usually
    stationary) could be used in the plays.

Ludus	Assumption	p. 365, after	LC, fol. 219^r
Coventriae		line 285	
		p. 373, after	LC, fol. 222^v
		line 493	
Coventry	Drapers Accounts, fols. 35-36, 39		
Norwich	Grocers' Accounts, 1534		

PIPE
    This could be any number of instruments: the shawm (a
    double-reed pipe with conical tube and expanding bell), the
    hornpipe (a single-reed pipe), the bagpipe, or a simple
    whistle.

Chester	Late Banns	p. 6, line 118	B, fol. 1^v
			R, fol. 2^v
Chester	Shepherds	p. 157, after	B, fol. 60^v
		line 606	D, fol. 48^v
			H, omitted
			R, fol. 65^v
			W, fol. 55^v
Coventry	Shearmen & Taylors' Play	p. 11, line 310	
Coventry	Smiths' Accounts, 1477		
York	Mercers' Indenture, 1433		

REGAL
    A type of organ with one or more reed pipes.

| Chester | Smiths' Accounts | BL, Harl. 2054, fol. 18^v |

Coventry   Drapers'
                 Accounts, fols.
                 36-89, *passim*

Coventry   Weavers'
                 Accounts, fols.
                 43^r-71^r, *passim*

TABARTE

A shallow drum with two parchment heads, beaten with a
stick or the hands.

Chester   Late Banns   p. 6, line 118   B, fol. 1^v
                                                                R, fol. 2^v

TRUMPET, TRUMPE

A metal tube of cylindrical bore opening at the end to a
broader bell. As it grew longer, it was frequently folded
into an "S"-shape.

Coventry   Shearmen and   p. 19, line 538
                 Taylors' Play

Coventry   Drapers'
                 Accounts, fols.
                 15-89, *passim*

Towneley   Judgment   p. 370, line 107   T, fol. 123^r

York   Mercers' Inden-
                 ture, 1433

                 Mercers' Accounts,
                 1526

TUBA

The Chester stage direction gives this term for the translation of "beam." Presumably the York reference does so as
well.

Chester   Judgment   p. 428, after   B, fol. 166^v
                                   line 40   D, fol. 142^v
                                                    H, fol. 131^v
                                                    R, fol. 194^v
                                                    W, fol. 162^r

York	Corporation		A/Y, fol.
	Memorandum Book		254^V
	with reference to		
	the Judgment play		

VIOL

A bowed, guitar-shaped instrument held between the knees, and having five or six strings.

| Coventry | Shearmen and | p. 19, line 538 |
| | Taylors' Play | |

WHISTLE

A recorder-type, vertical pipe with a thumb hole at the back as well as holes at the front.

Chester	Painters'
	Accounts, 1568,
	fol. 35^V

WIND INSTRUMENTS

Ludus	Adoration of	p. 152, line 19	LC, fol. 92^r
Coventriae	the Magi		
	Massacre of	p. 174, line 153	LC, fol. $102^{'}$
	the Innocents		
	Death of Herod	p. 176, lines	LC, fol. 104^1
		231-32.	
	Death of Herod	p. 176, after	LC, fol. 104^r
		line 232	

V.   COMMENTARY ON INDEX OF INSTRUMENTS

Far fewer indications for instrumental music than for
vocal music are provided by the play texts. Only six plays
from all the cycles (three from Chester, and three from the
Ludus Coventriae) direct that minstrels shall play; only eleven
different instruments are mentioned.

The second Chester play, dealing with the creation and
fall of man, has five indications of minstrelsy included in all
manuscripts but H, and B alone adds yet another.[1] The omission
in H of any references to minstrels' music in this play is
surely another instance of the purifying zeal of the scribe
who frequently "improved" the songs in the section of the
manuscript he copied.[2]

Minstrels are directed to play again in the Chester Magi
play,[3] but neither in this direction nor those in the Creation
play are the instruments which are to be played described. In
the Banns of 1475, however, the author has enjoined the Smiths
to "Get mynstrilles to that shewe, pipe, tabarte and flute."[4]
That wind instruments were the frequent choice of the minstrels
is suggested by the three directions in the *Ludus Coventriae*:
Herod tells his minstrels to "blowe up a good blast," and the
same phrase is used by the Seneschal, "blowe up mynstrall,"
and by Herod again, "blowe up a mery fytt."[5] The description
of the resulting action uses the verb "buccinant," indicating a number of minstrels playing trumpets of some type.

Of the instruments mentioned in the plays, winds of
various sorts predominate. The Chester First Shepherd blows
a *cornu*,[6] the angels in the Chester, Towneley, and York Judgment plays blow "beams," which the Chester scribes call
tubas.[7] A Towneley demon, after hearing the instrument, comments, "It was like to a trumpe/ it had sich a sownde. . . ."[8]
The music of trumpets is mentioned in the Coventry Shearmen
and Taylors' play, when Herod calls for "Trompettis, viallis,
and othur armone. . . ."[9] The simplest of the wind instruments is the gift of one of the Chester shepherd boys to the
Christ Child; he gives his pipe whose music could make the
"wood . . . ring/ and quiver. . . ."[10]

Bells are required in the Towneley and Coventry plays
dealing with the purification of Mary, and since the action

requires the representation of the Temple bells ringing in
jubilant welcome, they probably would be more elaborate than
handbells. Simeon, in the Towneley play, exclaims:

> A, dere god! what may this be?
> Oure bellys ryng so solemply . . .
> Oure bellys ryng by thare oone.[11]

In the Coventry play, the ringing of the bells is the prelude
to the procession that Simeon leads to greet the Christ Child.[12]

Only two plucked instruments are named, and one of them
may not be played. David in the Towneley Prophets sings "a
fytt,/ With [his] minstrelsy," and describes it as "myrth I
make till all men,/ with my harp and fyngers ten . . . ,"[13] but
he may be merely holding the instrument, not actually performing on it, since the figure of David the Psalmist with his harp
is a commonplace in iconography. The citharas played by the
angels in the *Ludus Coventriae* Assumption are also familiar
from illuminations and statues, but here the direction is clear
that the instruments are played by what the angel has called
the "hefnely consorcyte": "hic discendet angelus ludentibus
citharis."[14]

Only two textual references to the organ occur, those in
the *Ludus Coventriae* Assumption: "hic cantabunt organa" and
"cantantibus organis."[15] These stage directions were part of
the evidence marshalled by Hardin Craig to show that the
Assumption play was the production described in Lincoln
Cathedral records as performed in the nave by the members of
the chapter: "it is also to be observed that an organ is
called for in the Hegge play, so that that play either was or
had been played in church."[16] Professor Craig was not aware,
apparently, that portative organs could also have been used
and, hence, that musical considerations alone need not have
entailed a performance inside a church.

The only instruments mentioned in connection with the
plays in the various account books of guilds are the whistles
provided for the four shepherd boys in the Chester Painters'
play, trumpets used in the Coventry Drapers' and York Mercers'
plays, regals played in the Coventry Drapers' and Weavers'
plays, and the organ of the Norwich Grocers' play.[17]

Where, however, waits are included in the guilds' expenditures on music, other instruments, either those bought by
the corporations for their musicians, or those belonging to
the musicians themselves, can be suggested as having been
used in the plays. The Chester Waits, paid by the Smiths in
1571, had in their possession "howboies" (ancestors of the
oboe), recorders, "cornetes and violens"[18] by 1590, and among

the goods and chattels listed in William Madock's 1604 will
were a "sagbutt" (the medieval trombone) valued at thirteen
shillings and four pence, a "dubble certull" (probably an
early form of the bassoon) worth ten shillings, two "cor-
nettes" at five shillings each, and a "tenor wiall" (viol),
assessed at six shillings and eight pence.[19]

Coventry's Wardens paid in 1575 for a bass pipe to aug-
ment their waits' instruments; the waits had been hired for
the Smiths' Pageant from the fifteenth century.[20] Records
that recount the hiring of waits for the plays in Norwich
and York do not exist, but it can be assumed the men were
present as performers. Their instruments varied, for in York
in 1566 they possessed "a noise of four shalmes"[21] (early
types of oboe), while in Norwich, the Chamberlains in 1569
paid seventy-five shillings for iij [new] pypes for the waytes,"
and by 1585, their instruments included "ij Trompettes, iiij
Sagguebuttes, iij haukboyes, v Recorders, beeyng a whoall
noyse, vj Flagges [whistle flutes], one old Lyzardyne [a
cornett the length of which entailed its being coiled
together]."[22]

Since waits were employed by the Corporations of the
cities in which they served, they were called upon to perform
on civic occasions, the most magnificent of which were royal
entries. From contemporary descriptions of the musical welcome given the visiting royalty, more information about waits'
instruments and instruments generally used for street pageants
can be obtained.

In 1474, Prince Edward visited Coventry, and the Leet
Book gives a detailed description of the welcome he received.
Speeches and tributes were delivered at each of five stations,
and music formed part of the elaborate display: at Bablake
Gate was "mynstrallcy of the Waytes of the City," at the
Conduit, "mynstralcy of harpe and dowsemeris," at the Broad-
gate, "mynstrelcy of harpe & lute," at Cross Cheaping, "mynstrelcy of small pypis," and at the Crosscheaping Conduit,
"mynstrelcy of Orgon pleyinge."[23]

Coventry was the scene of another royal entry in 1498,
when Prince Arthur visited the city. Although the pageants
were just as elaborate as those which had welcomed Prince
Edward, the details of the musical segments of each station
are not so extensive. Instruments are mentioned at only one
of the four stations, that at Cross Cheaping, where there
were "angels sensying & syngyng, with Orgayns and othere
Melody etc."[24]

Since the waits at any one time numbered only from three
to five men, additional musicians would have had to be found
for such royal entries, and especially for performances of the

mystery plays. The need for more musicians could be met in several ways: members of the guild who could play instruments were hired, as at Norwich, where John Bakyn, a grocer, played the regals for his craft's production. That non-professional musicians such as Bakyn were not necessarily second-rate performers is suggested by the terms of apprenticeship, overseen by the searchers of the guild, of Thomas Knott, identured to Michael Knott, mason of Norwich, in 1559: Thomas is to learn "to pley in and uppon the vyoll vyolletts and harpe as allso to synge playne songe & pryksong. . . ." At the end of the apprenticeship he is to be given "a sufficient vyoll a vyolet and a harpe one trowell on plumbe rewle on handaxe on square and doble apparell etc in wollen & lynnen etc."[25]

If the waits of a city did not have a monopoly, independent musicians residing there could be hired, as the payments in the Chester guild accounts testify. William Luter and Rand Crane, for example, were two Chester minstrels who played for the Smiths.[26]

Whether travelling musicians, those minstrels who wandered from town to town until vagabondage acts restricted them, were hired to provide music for the productions of the mystery cycles is, however, another matter. The hiring of "minstrels" is a common enough entry in all the accounts available for study, but were these minstrels merely performers who, in the expectation of having a job, flocked to cities that were producing cycles? Such could not have been the case in York from at least 1561 when the ordinances of the Minstrels' Guild were passed, for the first rule forbade any foreigner to engage in performing or singing within the city.[27] Evidently the York minstrels felt that their own numbers were sufficient not only to produce their play of Herod and the Magi, but to supply the music for the other plays as well.[28]

The statutes of the York minstrels seem to have been the most restrictive with respect to the hiring of "foreigners," for Beverley's minstrels' guild could admit as brothers the minstrels of noblemen, waits of other corporations, and any musician proving himself to be capable.[29] The only law regulating the minstrels residing in Cheshire was that they be licensed at the annual court held by the Duttons of Dutton; with a whole county from which to draw, the Chester plays would be certain to be supplied with enough instrumentalists.[30] Coventry seems to have had no monopolistic ordinances, whether on behalf of its own waits, or any of the resident musicians.

The types of music all these musicians played can only

be a matter for speculation, since none survives in the plays, nor can the extant instrumental music of the period be shown to possess any connection with the cycles. The dramatic context, however, permits some general suggestions to be made about what the music might have been.

Fanfares of various sorts occur in the plays: the Last Judgment is announced by angels blowing beams, and the banquet of Herod and his court is brought in with a ceremonial fanfare to mark the service of the courses.[31] Although the angelic "blowing up" would obviously have no actual analogues, horn and trumpet announcements of royalty would be no novelty to inhabitants of most English cities;[32] even the opening of the Assizes might very well be considered as a kind of mundane reckoning whose ceremonial, transferred to the Judgment play, would be immediately recognizable. The accompaniment of the courses of a lavish banquet with fanfares found its most spectacular expression at Henry VIII's coronation:

> . . . at the bryngyng of the first course, the
> trumpettes blew up. And in came the Duke of
> Buckyngham, mounted upon a greate courser, richeley
> trapped and embroudered, and the lorde Stewarde, in·
> likewise on an horse, trapped in clothe of golde,
> ridyng before the service, which was sumpteous. . . .[33]

In contrast to the sophistication of formal fanfares are the horn blasts of the Chester First Shepherd, really little more than signals to his comrades. But even here, an actor with musical skill (or a minstrel hidden from the audience's view) could blow an identifiable call taken, for example, from a hunt or similar entertainment, or even a huntsup itself.[34]

If the four whistles purchased for the Chester shepherd boys were played, the music would undoubtedly have been of a rustic simplicity suitable not only to the instruments, but also to the characters played by the boys. One presumes that the "pipe" of the play and the whistle of the accounts are synonymous, and refer to a recorder-type of instrument.[35] The Chester Smiths also required a pipe, but in conjunction with a "tabarte and flute."[36] The instrument meant here is probably either a bagpipe or a shawm. Whichever was used, the performance would seem to require only two men: the pipe-player and the agile "tabor piper," who would play the flute with the left hand and beat the tabor with his right. Such music was associated with country dances, especially morris dances in England, but one would be presumptuous to infer from this the presence of dancing in every play where dance music could be performed.[37]

The joyful peals of the Temple bells welcoming the Christ Child in the Coventry and Towneley Purification plays[38] would not require other than straightforward musical means. Exuberance rather than complex changes would be called for, although again, if the performer had the skill, enthusiasm and musicality could be combined to good effect.

The foregoing are examples of instrumental music performed and heard in itself. Instrumental music as accompaniment is also present in the cycles. Whether or not the Towneley David played his harp, his purpose in having it was to accompany his song in what could be, if actually played, improvised doubling of the voice part, or rhythmic punctuation.[39]

The regals played by James Hewett at Coventry and the organ by John Bakyn at Norwich[40] were not intended to be solo instruments, but support for the songs in the play--the elaborateness of the support depending, quite obviously, on the skill of the performer. In the case of James Hewett, an accomplished musician, one suspects the accompaniment to have been the equal of the singing.

In the *Ludus Coventriae* Assumption, however, the organ and citharas one would expect to be used as accompaniment for the angelic choir seem instead to perform as principal instruments.[41] The organist would have had a large liturgical repertory from which to choose, either a melody originally for voices upon which to improvise, or, by this late fifteenth-century date, music written specifically for the organ.[42] The citharists, if indeed the stage direction is accurate and no song was intended, would probably have played, since they are angels, an intabulation of some liturgical piece.

The minstrels of the Chester and *Ludus Coventriae* plays could have played almost any music, depending on their ability and instruments.[43] It seems safe to assume that the Chester Creation music would have been recognizably liturgical since it accompanies the comings and goings of God, but the music in the Magi plays of the two cycles as well as that in the banquet scene of the *Ludus Coventriae* Innocents must have been completely secular, since in each case Herod's court is being presented. If the musicians were familiar with the practices of their own royalty at feasts, the music may have been authentic "dinner music," or at least of the same character.[44]

What seems to be an arrangement of instruments that groups them with no regard to their sonority is illustrated in the Herod section of the Coventry Shearmen and Taylors' play. The king asks for "trompettis, viallis, and othur

armone . . . ,"[45] a combination which unites loud and soft
instruments in the same consort. Such a mixture is unexpected,
for, as Edmund Bowles remarks:

> It was [the] esthetic tendency to think of instru-
> ments in terms of volume that led to the dual group-
> ing according to sonority; those instruments with a
> loud, shrill tone color (*haut*), and those whose
> sound was soft, or low (*bas*). . . . The majority
> of these events [using orchestral performances, such
> as liturgical services, mystery plays, banquet
> festivities, and dances] displayed a rather rigid
> and invariable distinction between the two group-
> ings.[46]

It is, therefore, of interest to note that the strict division
of instruments into *haut* and *bas* did not always obtain, and
that the variety of possible sonorities benefitted as a
result.

That the play texts alone are not sufficient for an
accurate judgment to be made about the instrumental music
used in the plays is apparent from the supplemental information revealed by the guild accounts, few though they are.
Logic can lead even further; for example, although there is
not one indication of music in the Minstrels' Play at York
as given in the manuscript, and no guild books survive, it
is inconceivable that the production should not have been
full of music. The York Minstrels' Play may have been an
exception; the music would, of course, vary in amount and
quality from play to play, and from city to city. But, in
general, one can say that the documentary evidence provides
a tantalizing glimpse of what must have been a widespread
and varied use of instrumental music in the plays.

VI. GLOSSARY OF MUSICAL TERMS

The following Glossary is divided into two sections, the
first containing words that have a specifically musical meaning, the second containing words that describe the music performed in the plays. The terms of Part II are treated only
summarily since their inclusion is on the basis of their
association with the words listed in Part I; they are de-
fined if their meanings might be doubtful. When a word such
as "song" or "minstrel" occurs in a great number of plays, a
single location in each cycle is given.

Because the Glossary is limited to a list of musical
terms found in the mystery plays, complete lexicographical
information is not presented. I have, however, made extensive use of Carter's *Dictionary of Middle English Musical
Terms* and the *Middle English Dictionary* to verify from
other vernacular sources the musical meanings implied by the
usage of the words in the cycles.

PART I

ANTEM, sb. [OE antef(e)n; L antiphona], Either a term trans-
lating ANTIPHONA (see below), or a vernacular religious
composition.

Coventry, Weavers' Play, 58.after 805: The syng an
antem.

ANTIPHONA, sb., (1) a plainchant composition usually based on
a scriptural text, sung before and after, and sometimes
between, the verses of a psalm; (2) processional antiphons
with texts from the New Testament; (3) the four Marian
antiphons sung during the year at the end of Compline.
The York reference is to one of the latter.

York, Death of Mary, 479.after 194: Et cantant antiphona scilicet Ave regina celorum.

ARMONY, sb. (also ARMONE) [L harmonia], The act of singing or
making music; music or song.

Coventry, Shearmen and Taylors, 10.267: draw we nere/ To
here there armony; ibid., 19.538: Trompettis, viallis,
and other armone.

BASS, sb. [OF bas], The lowest of men's voices; here, the
lowest part of a polyphonic composition.

Norwich, Fall of Man B, 18.after 153: Old Musick
Triplex, Tenor, Medius, Bass.

BLAST, sb. [OE blæst], The sound of a wind instrument, or the
act of blowing it.

Chester, Judgment, 429.46: thy Bames blast hath raysed
me; Ludus Coventriae, Magi, 152.19: ȝe mynstrell of
myrth blowe up a good blast; Towneley, Prophets, 62.201:
ffull sorowfull shall be that blast; ibid., Judgment,
368.41: Alas, I am forlorne!/ a spytus blast here
blawes.

BREFES, sb. [OF brief, bref; L brevis], The name of a note
having the time value of two or three semibreves, and
one-half or one-third of a long. This is one of the
first known English uses of the word. Towneley, Second
Shepherds, 137.657: Thre brefes to a long.

BREK, vb. [OE brecan], To sing; to begin to sing.

Towneley, First Shepherds, 113.422: Brek outt youre
voce/ let se as ye yelp.

BUCCINANT, vb., To blow on the trumpet, and perhaps other wind
instruments.

Ludus Coventriae, Herod, 176.after 232: Hic dum buccinant
mors interficiat herodem.

CANTARE, vb., To sing; to play on an instrument.

Chester, Noah, 58.after 256: Tunc Noe claudet fenestram
Archae et per modicum spatium infra tectum cantent
psalmum; Coventry, Weavers, 45.366: Cantant; Ludus
Coventriae, Betrothal, 91.after 300: Et hic cantent.
Benedicta sit beata trinitas; ibid., Assumption,

365.after 285: hic cantabunt organa; ibid., 373.after
493: Et hic assendent in celum cantantibus organis;
Towneley, Harrowing, 294.after 44: Et cantent omnes
"saluator mundi"; York, Creation, 2.after 24: Tunc
cantant angeli Te deum.

CANTUS, sb., Song or melody.

York, Judgment, 505.after 216: Hic ad sedem iudicij cum
cantu angelorum.

CARMEN, sb., A song, the text of which is probably a poem in
the vernacular.

Chester, Shepherds, 151.after 458: Tunc omnes pastores
cum aliis adiuvantibus cantabunt hilare carmen.

CHAUNTT, vb. [OF cha(u)nter], To sing; here, probably without
any religious connotation.

Towneley, Second Shepherds, 122.189: lett se how ye
chauntt.

CONSORCYTE, sb. [OF consorcieté], A musical group or company.

Ludus Coventriae, Assumption, 358.90: Ffor qwyche
message injoyeth the hefnely consorcyte.

CRAK, vb. [OE cracian, cf. OHG krahhon], To sing; also to
divide into notes of short time value.

Towneley, First Shepherds, 131.477: hard I neuer none
crak/ so clere out of toyne; ibid., Second Shepherds,
137.656: Say, what was his song?/ hard ye not how he
crakyd it?; York, Shepherds, 120.67; I have so crakid
in my throte.

CROCHETT, sb. [OF crochett], The name of a note now our quarter note, probably the value of the fifteenth-century
semiminima; one of the first known uses of this word in
English.

Towneley, Second Shepherds, 137.658: was no crochett
wrong.

CROYNE, vb. [cf. MDu cronen, OHG kronen], Generally, to sing
or hum softly, but it can mean, in Northern dialect,

"to roar like a bull"(Cawley, p. 110, fn. 476); hence, the scornful reference to Mak's song.

> Towneley, First Shepherds, 131.476: will ye here how thay hak?/ oure syre, lyst, croyne; ibid., Second Shepherds, 137.661: let se how ye croyne; ibid., Talents, 281.67: nawder with cryyng nor with cronyng.

CURIOSE, adj. [OF curius], Ornate, elaborate; also skillful and expert; and sophisticated and recondite.

> Towneley, First Shepherds, 110.306: that sang . . . was wonder curiose/ with small noytys emang.

DECANTENT, vb., To sing forth, to sing with enthusiasm.

> *Ludus Coventriae*, Noah, 43.after 253: Hic decantent hos versus.

DIRIGE, sb. [L vb. dirige], Office of the Dead, from the incipit "Dirige, Domine," the first antiphon of Matins for that Office.

> *Ludus Coventriae*, Assumption, 362.195: saynge my dirige · devouthly and sad; ibid., 365.289: wyth the hefnely quer yowre dirige to rede.

DRAWES, vb. [OE dragan], To play an instrument, especially a horn; to play or blow slowly.

> Towneley, Judgment, 368.42: I harde well bi yonde horne/ I wote wherto it drawes.

FLABUNT, vb. (FLAT), To blow on a wind instrument.

> Chester, Shepherds, 134.after 48: Tunc flat cum Cornu; ibid., Judgment, 428.after 40: Tunc Angeli Tubas accipient et flabunt.

FITT, sb. [OE fit(t)], A section of a poem or song, the precise length of which is uncertain; a melody or song.

> *Ludus Coventriae*, Herod, 176.232: blowe up a mery fytt; Towneley, Prophets, 59.104: shall I now syng you a fytt; ibid., 61.157: Now haue I songen you a fytt.

GENTYLL, adj. [OF gentil; L gentilis], Soft and pleasing; see

SMALL, with which it forms a common epithet.

Towneley, First Shepherds, 113.418: Thay were gentyll and small.

GLEE, sb. (gle) [OE glēo], Music of a joyful kind; a musical performance.

Chester, Shepherds, 148.393: it was "Glorum, glarum" with a glee; Towneley, First Shepherds, 110.326: It was a mery gle.

HAK, vb. (HAKT) [OE haccian], To divide a note into notes of smaller time value.

Towneley, Second Shepherds, 131.476: will ye here how thay hak? ibid., 137.657: yee, mary, he hakt it.

HIGHT, sb. [OE hyht], Joy; therefore, to sing joyfully. Or from OE hīgþ; hence, promptly?

Towneley, First Shepherds, 116.498: syng we therto on hight.

HYMPNE, sb. [OE ymen; OF ymne; L (h)ym(p)nus], A hymn, i.e., a religious song of praise composed of a number of stanzas each of which is sung to the same tune.

Ludus Coventriae, Mary in the Temple, 81.after 259: þei xal synge in hefne þis hympne.

KNAKT, vb. [MDu cna(c)ken, cf. MHG knacken, gnacken], To divide notes into those of smaller time value; hence, to sing in a florid style.

Towneley, Second Shepherds, 137.659: ffor to syng vs emong/ right as he knakt it,/ I can.

LAUDE, sb. and vb. (LAWDE) [OF laude; L laudes], A song of praise; to sing such a piece of music.

Chester, Nativity, 107.68: and lawde to his lykinge; ibid., Purification, 211.165-66: therfore a songe, as I haue tighte,/ and laudes to thee; Towneley, First Shepherds, 116.501-02: To the lawde of this lam/ Syng we in syght.

LEDDEN, sb. [OE lǣdan], The musical sounds (or melody) peculiar to a particular song. Or perhaps "Latin," influenced by leden, language?

Chester, Shepherds, 150.429: such a ledden . . . never in my life me so lyked.

LOFT, sb. [ON (á) lopt], To sing loudly, clearly.

Towneley, Second Shepherds, 140.753-54: To syng ar we bun:/ let take on loft.

LONG, sb. [L longa], The name of a note whose value equals two or three breves and one-half or one-third of a maxima. The first known use of this word in English seems to be in the Towneley plays.

Towneley, First Shepherds, 113.414: I dar say that he broght/ foure & twenty to a long; ibid., Second Shepherds, 137.657: Thre brefes to a long.

LUDENTIBUS, vb. form, The playing of musical instruments.

Ludus Coventriae, Assumption, 358.after 90: hic discendet angelus ludentibus citharis.

MEDIUS, sb., A middle part in a polyphonic composition, Cf. MEYN.

Norwich, Fall of Man B, 18.after 153: Old Musick Triplex, Tenor, Medius, Bass.

MELODIA, see MELODY.

MELODY, sb. (MELODYE) [OF melodie; L melodia], A combination of musical sounds, a song or tune.

Chester, Nativity, 107.67: with joifull mirth and melodye; *Ludus Coventriae*, Judgment, 375.56: Where myrthe and melody nevyr may mys; Towneley, Resurrection, 322.522: we hard neuer . . . sich melody; York, Judgment, 513.after 380: Et sic facit finem cum melodia angelorum.

MEYN, sb. (MEYNE) [OF meien, L medianus], A middle part in a polyphonic song or instrumental piece.

Towneley, Second Shepherds, 122.188: Then the meyne
fallys to me; ibid., Judgment, 384.537: The meyn shall
ye nebyll.

MYNSTRALL, sb. (MINSTRELS, MYNSTRILLES, MINSTRELSY) [OF
menestrel; L minister, ministerialis], Musicians; a
musical performance.

Chester, Creation, 24.fn. for 112: minstrels (mynstrilles) play; *Ludus Coventriae*, Herod, 174.153: now
blowe up mynstrall with all ȝour myght; Towneley,
Prophets, 59.104-05: shall I now syng you a fytt,/
With my minstrelsy.

MYRTH, sb. (MIRTHE) [OE myrth, myrgþ], To perform music; a
melody or song.

Chester, Shepherds, 152.487-88: and sing we all, I
redd,/ some myrth to his maiesty; Towneley, Prophets,
60.109: Myrth I make till all men; ibid., Judgment,
387.619: Make we all myrth and louyng; York, Shepherds,
122.131: And make mirthe as we gange.

MUSIQUE, sb. (MUSYKE, MUSICK) [OF musique; L musica], A
vocal or instrumental performance; the art, science, or
study of tones.

Chester, Shepherds, 151.458: for musique of me learne
you may; *Ludus Coventriae*, Doctors, 178.11: of Swete
musyke; Norwich, Fall of Man A, 10.after 80: Musick;
ibid., 11.after 90; These last 2 lines set to musick;
ibid., Fall of Man B, 18.after 153: Old Musick, Triplex, Tenor, Medius, Bass.

MUTING, vb. (MEWTED) [L mutire?; OE mǣw?], To sing quietly?
To sing with a high-pitched sound?

Chester, Shepherds, 147.371: this muting on height;
ibid., 150.431: upon "hominibus" he mewted.

NEBYLL, vb. [MLG nibbelen]. To try to sing.

Towneley, First Shepherds, 384.537: The meyn shall ye
nebyll.

NEOWELL, sb. [OF nowel], A word sung as a refrain in celebration of Christ's birth.

Coventry, Shearmen & Taylors, 16.474: And there songe
hit ys "Neowell."

NOYSE, sb. (NOISE) [OF noise], Pleasant musical sounds.

Coventry, Shearmen & Taylors, 10.278: Now, Lorde, this
noise that I do here; Towneley, Purification, 184.109:
This noyse lyghtyns full well myn hart; ibid., 185.113:
ffor sich noyse hard I neuer ere; York, Shepherds,
120.71: That tille vs made þis noble noyse.

NOTA, see NOTE

NOTE, sb. (NOTA, NOYTYS) [OF note; L nota], A character or
sign in written music; a tone in heard music; a melody
or tune.

Chester, Shepherds, 148.396: me thought that note went
ouer the howse; ibid., 149.426: that note on height when
he up hente; ibid., Nativity, 130.after 680: fiat nota
secundum arbitrium agentis; Towneley, First Shepherds,
110.306: It was wonder curiose/ with small noytys
emang; York, Shepherds, 120.65: Ha! Ha! þis was a mery
note.

ORGANA, sb., The term probably refers to an organ, either por-
table or stationary, rather than to polyphony of a very
early type, or to instruments in general.

Ludus Coventriae, Assumption, 365.after 285: hic
cantabunt organa; ibid., 373.after 493: Et hic assendent
in celum cantantibus organis.

PIPED, vb. [OE pīpian], By transference from the instrument,
to sing with a clear high sound.

Chester, Shepherds, 150.428: up as pie he piped.

PLAIE, vb. [OE plegan, plegian], To make music on an instrument.

Chester, Magi, 166.fn. for 144: the mynstrilles mvste
plaie.

PSALME, sb. [OE sealm, psalm; OF salme, psaume; L psalmus],
One of the Old Testament songs of David; by transfer-

ence, any devotional composition, here referring to the
two New Testament canticles, the "Magnificat" and the
"Nunc Dimittis."

Ludus Coventriae, Purification, 167.after 146: The
psalme songyn every vers; ibid., Visitation, 120.105:
This psalme of prophesye seyd be-twen vs tweyn.

PULSABUNT, vb., To strike or beat; by transference, the
ringing of bells.

Towneley, Purification, 184.after 102: Tunc pulsabunt.

QUER, sb. (QUERE) [OF cuer; L chorus], A group of singers;
more specifically, angelic singers.

Ludus Coventriae, Assumption, 365.289: Wyth the
hefneley quer yowre dirige to rede; Coventry, Shearmen
& Taylors, 9.265: Hard I neyuer of soo myrre a quere.

REVANT, sb.? The meaning of this word is uncertain. Perhaps it is a scribal error for "tenour," the third voice
of the devils' trio.

Towneley, Judgment, 384.539: A revant the devill.

SCREMYD, vb. (SKREME, sb.) [OE scrӡman], To sing loudly,
probably in the upper register.

Towneley, First Shepherds, 110.310: Oone scremyd on
lowde; ibid., 110.328: As he sayde in a skreme.

SEQUENCIAM, see SEQUENS

SEQUENS, sb. (SEQUENCIAM) [L sequens, sequential], A liturgical song in which the same melody is stated for each
of two rhyming lines; the melody of every pair differs,
viz., a bb cc . . . ff g.

Ludus Coventriae, Conception of Mary, 65.after 72:
There they xal synge þis sequens; ibid., Annunciation,
108.after 340; Angeli cantando istam sequenciam.

SHEWTED, vb. [ON skúta, skúte, sb.], To shout or utter sounds
loudly; by transference, to sing loudly.

Chester, Shepherds, 150.433: And aye I quocke while he
so shewted.

SYGHT, sb. [OE gesiht], A method of singing polyphony in
which one part sings a given melody, while the other two
improvise "at sight" parallel countermelodies according
to fixed rules.

Towneley, First Shepherds, 116.502: Syng we in syght.

SYNG, vb. (SINGE, SYNGE) [OE singan], To produce music by means
of the human voice.

Chester, Nativity, 107.72: deuoutlie I will sing; Coventry, Shearmen & Taylors, 9.after 263: There the angelis
syng "Glorea in exselsis Deo"; *Ludus Coventriae*, Trial of
Mary, 129.164: Ffayr chylde lullay sone must she syng;
Towneley, Second Shepherds, 137.659: ffor to syng vs
emong; York, Entry into Jerusalem, 209.265: Go synge
before.

SMALL, adj., [OE smæl], Quiet and of low volume, see GENTYLL
with which it forms a common epithet; also, of short
duration.

Towneley, First Shepherds, 113.418: Thay were gentyll
and small; ibid., 110.306: It was wonder curiose/ with
small noytys emang.

SONG, sb. (SONGE, SANGRE, SANGE) [OE sang, song], The music
produced by a human voice; a piece of music to be performed by the human voice.

Chester, Abraham, 78.350: my song may be "well awaye!"
Coventry, Shearmen & Taylors, 10.269: For be the
swettnes of ther songe; *Ludus Coventriae*, Banns, 1.18:
Than Angell with songe þis is no nay; Towneley, First
Shepherds, 113.430: Take at my sangre; ibid., 137.656:
Say, what was his song; York, Pentecost, 469.132: þat
sais þus in þer sange.

SOWDE, vb. [OE swōgan], To sing gently but penetratingly.

Towneley, First Shepherds, 110.312: In myn erys it
sowde.

STEVEN, sb. (STEVYN, STEVENE) [OE stefn], A musical voice or
sound.

Ludus Coventriae, Shepherds, 146.7: Therfore I synge A

joyful stevene; Towneley, First Shepherds, 113.409:   I
hard by hys steuen; ibid., Second Shepherds, 137.647:
This was a qwant stevyn.

TAMED, vb. [OF tamer], To commence, begin, venture upon a
song or part of a song.

Chester, Shepherds, 150.443:   and that word "terra" he
tamed.

TENORY, sb. [OF tenor; L tenor], The voice usually taken or
adapted from another source and acting as the main
structural element in early polyphony.   Here the term
has the additional meaning of the lowest voice.

Towneley, Second Shepherds, 122.186:   lett me syng the
tenory.

TOYN, sb. (TOYNE, TONYD, vb.) [OF ton; L tonus], To sing in
such a way that the sound produced is pleasing; to sing
with correct pitch; a tune or melody.

Towneley, First Shepherds, 113.419:   Thay were . . .
well tonyd with all; ibid., Second Shepherds, 131.477:
hard I neuer none crak/ so clere out of toyne; ibid.,
Flight into Egypt, 161.13:   so swete of toyn.

TREBILL, sb. (TRYBLE) [OF treble; L triplus], The highest voice,
or second highest if there is a quatreble, in a polyphonic composition.

Towneley, Second Shepherds, 122.187:   And I the tryble so
hye; ibid., Judgment, 384.538:   And I shall syng the
trebill.

TRIPLEX, sb., In a polyphonic composition, a part above the
tenor.

Cf. TREBILL.

Norwich, Fall of Man B, 18.after 153:   Old Musick Triplex,
Tenor, Medius, Bass.

UNYSOUNE, sb. [L unisonus],   The "interval" formed by a tone
and its duplication; by transference, in the York play,
to sing in agreement and concord.

York, Entry into Jerusalem, 209.262: With braunches,
floures, and unysoune,/ With myghtfull songes.

VOYCE, sb. (VOYS, VOCE) [OF vois; L vox], A voice considered
   especially with respect to its musical quality; the
   performance of vocal music.

   Chester, Shepherds, 149.417: he had a much better voyce
   then had I; *Ludus Coventriae*, Shepherds, 149.80: I
   haue þat voys fful wele I wote; Towneley, First Shepherds,
   113.422: Brek outt youre voce/ let se as ye yelp.

YELP, vb. [OE gelpan], To sing loudly, or on high notes.

   Towneley, First Shepherds, 113.422: let se as ye yelp.

PART II

(to sing) BOLDLY   Towneley, Judgment, 387.617

(to sing) DEVOWTLY   Chester, Nativity, 107.72

DULCITER (cantabunt)   *Ludus Coventriae*, Assumption,
                                367.after 342.

DULLFULL (song)   Norwich, Fall of Man A, 10.88

(to blow) FAST   Chester, Judgment, 428.33

      to blow firmly, from OE fæste

GOOD (blast of a horn; see   *Ludus Coventriae*, Magi, 152.19
   BLAST, Part I)

HEDUS (song)   Towneley, Harrowing, 297.119

HYDYOUS (horn)   York, Judgment, 500.115

JOYFUL (songs)   *Ludus Coventriae*, Shepherds,
                                146.7

LOWDE, LOWT (of a horn)   Chester, Shepherds, 139.172
                                Towneley, First Shepherds,
                                110.310
      The loudness of an instrument

(to sing) MERELYE   Chester, Shepherds, 151.454

MERY (QUERE, Part I)   Coventry, Shearmen & Taylors,
                                 9.265
     (FITT, Part I)   *Ludus Coventriae*, Herod,
                                 176.232

     (songs)   York, Shepherds, 120.65
                                 Towneley, First Shepherds,
                                 110.326 and 113.413

MYGHTFULL (songs)   York, Entry into Jerusalem,
                                 209.263

Songs which have mighty themes? To sing with strength,
i.e., loudly and joyously?

NOBLE (NOYSE, Part I)   York, Shepherds, 120.71

QWANT (STEVEN, Part I)   Towneley, Second Shepherds,
                                 137.647

Curious and cunning; elegant and refined.

(to sing) SADLIE   Chester, Shepherds, 149.420

With deliberation, seriously.

SEMELY (songs)   York, Death of Mary, 479.194

(to sing) SHRILL   Chester, Shepherds, 151.453

With penetrating sounds.

(to sing with) SOLEMNITY   Chester, Harrowing, 329.260
                                 Coventry, Shearmen & Taylors,
                                 10.279
                                 York, Trial before Pilate,
                                 283.314

SORRY (songs)   Chester, Harrowing, 322.118;
                                 330.283
                                 Chester, Antichrist, 426.702
                                 York, Doctors, 157.43

SORROWFUL (songs)   Towneley, Prophets, 62.201

SPYTUS (BLAST, Part I)	Towneley, Judgment, 368.41
SWEETNESS (of a song)	Coventry, Shearmen & Taylors, 10.269
UGLY (NOYSE, Part I)	Towneley, Harrowing, 296.95

VII. COMMENTARY ON GLOSSARY OF MUSICAL TERMS

Words relating specifically to music are scattered throughout the mysteries, but nowhere in such abundance as in the Shepherds plays[1] in which the splendor of the angelic announcement calls forth from the herdsmen a corresponding brilliance of critical virtuosity.

The Chester Shepherds discuss at length, and most enthusiastically, the words of the angel's song; their account of the way in which he has sung is a piece of general descriptive criticism that, in the end, characterizes them.

GARTIUS.	Nay, it was "glore, glore glorius," me thought that note went ouer the howse. . . .
SECUNDUS PASTOR.	Naie, by my faith! it was a "gloria," said Gabriell, when he sang soe, he had a much better voice then had I, as in heaven all other haue so.
TERTIUS PASTOR.	will you heare how he sang "Celsis"? for on that sadlie he set hym. . . .
GARTIUS.	One tyme he touched upon "Tar," and ther I tooke good intent, all heaven might not have gone har, that note on height when he up hente.
PRIMUS PASTOR.	And after of "pax" or of peace up as pie he piped, such a ledden--this is no las-- never in my life me so lyked.
SECUNDUS PASTOR.	upon "hominibus" he mewted, that much marveyle to me was, And aye I quocke while he so shewted, I durst not hede wher that I was.[2]

We learn that the angel's voice was of such beauty as to excite great admiration, that in his song "Gloria" and "terra" (or "Tar," as Gartius puts it) were sung with high notes, that what could have been a melisma followed "pax." "Celsis" was longer in time value than what preceded it; "hominibus" was sung quietly. Perhaps the reference to high notes indicates that the "Gloria" was sung by a boy acting the angel's part.

Nothing about the description or the comparisons is sophisticated; neither are the shepherds, and their verbal reaction is an accurate representation of the way in which some people would respond to a thing so marvellous as an angel's song.

If the supposition is correct that this play's verse forms show evidence of revision,[3] the sections dealing with the reactions of the shepherds to the song of the angel suggest that the reviser's treatment of this customary episode is more subtle and more carefully thought out than that of the original version. In the early form (lines 369-410), the shepherds merely and comically fail to understand the angelic words; the reviser, however, has his shepherds describe the angelic song on three levels (411-46): first, that of the sound of the song, that is, the music; second, that of the meaning of the words, that is, the import of the song; and third, that of the effect that the music and words together have on the shepherds. Also, in this section alone in the cycles, the relationship of music and text is recognized and used figurally: the angel and the shepherds, the divine and the human, are essentially different, yet united through the event of the birth of Christ (435-46).

The Towneley Shepherds Plays are especially rich in musical vocabulary--that is, words which have a technical sense in music and which are used accurately and familiarly by the author. Whether shepherds would have such knowledge is questionable and their discussion may be out of character, but the terminology is used to express their wonderment at the complexity of the music of the angelic announcement rather than to vaunt any supposed erudition of their own.

The two plays differ in the nature of the shepherds' response to the music of the "Gloria." The comments in the First Shepherds' Play reveal a concern with the performance: "it was wonder curiose/ with small noytys emang . . . it was a mery gle." The shepherds elaborate on these two initial judgments:

> ij us pastor. Now, by god that me boght/ it was a mery song;
> I dar say that he broght/ foure & twenty to a
> long. . . .
> primus pastor. In fayth I trow noght/ so many he throng
> On a heppe;
> Thay were gentyll and small,
> And well tonyd with all. . . .

Although they are interested in the great number of notes, they are more struck by the quality of the performance of those notes:

> ij us pastor.   I hard by hys steuen,
> he was send downe ffro heuen.

> primus pastor.   It is trouth that ye neuen,
> I hard hym well spell.[4]

The Second Shepherds' Play also has a short passage describing the song, but the stress has shifted from awe at the beauty of the "Gloria" to wonder at the rhythmic complexity.

> ij us pastor.   Say, what was his song?/ herd ye not how he crakyd it?
> Thre brefes to a long./
> iij us pastor.   yee, mary, he hakt it.
> Was no crochett wrong/ nor no thyng that lakt it.
> primus pastor. ffor to syng vs emong/ right as he knakt it, I can.[5]

The three verbs "crakyd," "hakt," and "knakt" all refer to the dividing of a long note into notes of smaller value, and the rhythmic scheme of three breves to a long involves in its application precisely that procedure.

Medieval theorists schematized the temporal relationships between notes, their mensurations, into four "degrees": *maximodus* (the relationship between *maxima* and *longa* ⊏⊐ ☐),

modus (the relation between *longa* and *brevis* ☐ ☐), *tempus*

(*brevis* and *semibrevis* ☐ ◇), and *prolatio* (*semibrevis* and

minima ◇ ♭). A note equal to three smaller notes is called perfect; it is imperfect when it equals two smaller notes.[6] Hence, "thre brefes to a long" indicates that the *modus* is perfect, but to break the breves into even smaller divisions in order to reach "four & twenty to a long," the *tempus* and *prolatio* must both be imperfect, with an added imperfect

diminution (minima to semiminima ♭ ♦ or ♭) at the end to reach the necessary twenty-four: 3 (breves) x 2 (semibreves) x 2 (minims) x 2 (semiminims).

Moreover, the shepherds are aware not only of the basic rhythmic scheme; they have also noticed that the rhythm within the scheme—that involving the smaller note value of the "crochett"—is correct. Thus, the shepherds of the first play are impressed by the rhythmic scheme only insofar as it contributes to the florid style of the song. The second trio of shepherds, on the other hand, are struck by the rhythmic complexity itself and do not consider the song from the point of view of style, but merely as a "qwant stevyn."[7]

This difference in the general musical preoccupations of the shepherds is also shown in the way they describe their own singing. In the first play, the style of their songs is alluded to by "syng we in syght"; in the second, each man specifies the part he wishes to take in the song--tenor, mean, or treble.[8] Once again, the Second Shepherds' Play stresses the construction of the song, and the First Shepherds' Play implies the final sonorous outcome obtained from a particular method of singing.

Although it is described only in the one play, the style of the shepherds' singing would probably have been identical in both; hence, a dramatic contrast is created between their improvised and probably syllabic song and the ornate, technically complex melody of the angel--a contrast which opposes by implication, then, the supernatural character of the angel and the simple humanity of the shepherds. The intimate knowledge revealed in these plays of both musical style and musical technique as well as the use of purely musical means for a dramatic purpose are found nowhere else in the cycles, and provide additional justification for the assessment of the Wakefield Master, the author of both, as an artist and a "distinguished dramatist."[9]

Words which describe a musical performance but do not in themselves have a musical connotation occur rarely in the plays. The twenty-two terms falling into this category are of two sorts, those which relate to the nature of the songs, and those which deal with the performance. No unusual performance practices seem implied, although one wonders if the effect produced in singing "devowtly" and "with solemnity" did not rely more on the texts of the songs than on the way they were sung. When a song is called joyful or merry or seemly, the whole song--text and music--is obviously being considered, but to call a song "sweet" apparently refers in some way to its music alone. And surely one would expect the words, not the music, of a song to be "spytus"; yet, in the context of the Judgment Play in which the term appears, it is only music that is heard. Since the hearers are the damned, it is their self-knowledge and apprehension that make the meaning of the music, its significance, seem cruel. An effect produced by the music itself is less at issue than an effect produced because of the interior dispositions of the hearer.[10]

APPENDIX 1:
TRANSLATIONS

1. Receive the Holy Spirit: whose sins you forgive, they are forgiven them.

2. Our help is in the name of the Lord who has made heaven and earth.
   May the name of the Lord be blessed, now and forever to eternity.
   May the Divine Majesty and One God bless you: the Father, the Son, and the Holy Spirit. Amen.

3. Gracious chorus of the Lord, proclaim now the names of the Most High: messiah, savior, God-with-us, God of hosts, Lord.
   He is the only-begotten one, the way, the life, the power, the one-substance,
   The first principle, the first-born, wisdom, power,
   He is alpha and omega, he is called simultaneously beginning and end.
   The fount and source of good, comforter and intercessor, lamb, sheep, calf, serpent, ram, lion, worm, mouth, word, magnificence, sun, glory, light and likeness,
   bread, blossom, vine, mountain, door, rock, and jewel, spirit and spouse and shepherd, prophet, priest, death-destroyer, lord, divinity, omnipresent, omnipotent, equally-divided,
   He saves us: to him be glory for endless ages. Amen.

4. I ascend to my Father and your Father, to my God and your God. Alleluia.

5. Mary is assumed into heaven. The angels rejoice and, praising, bless the Lord.

6. Hail Mary full of grace. The Lord is with you, happy virgin.
   Blessed are you among women, you who gave birth to peace among men and the glory of angels.

And blessed is the fruit of your womb who has established
that we might be co-heirs with him through grace.
For this, moreover, hail: you brought an offspring so
sweetly into the world, contrary to the law of the flesh,
a new sun born from a new star.
You were the temple of Christ the Savior, of the great
lion and the little lamb, yet you remained a virgin.
You, queen of virgins, rose without a thorn, were made
mother of a flower and of the dew, of bread and a shepherd.
You are the city of the king of justice, the mother of
mercy;
You cause, by grace, the friend of God to be restored from
the pit of misery.
Therefore, star of the sea, sanctuary of the word of God
and dawning of the sun, gate of Paradise, through whom
light was born, pray to your Son that he forgive us our
sins and gather us together forever in the bright kingdom
in which [that] constant light shines. Amen.

7. Hail Queen of heaven, hail Lady of angels, hail holy root
    from whom a light for the world has risen. Hail glorious
    one, beautiful above all. Farewell, great in comeliness;
    and always [prevail upon] Christ for us.

8. All generations will call me blessed, because the Lord
    who is powerful, and holy is his name, has worked marvels
    for me.

9. Blessed be the holy Trinity, eternal God, in the glory
    of coequality.
    God the Father, equally the begotten Son, with the Holy
    Spirit abiding above all that exists.
    In whom is always one will and three persons, never
    disagreeing amongst themselves.
    For they are the same single God, not divided into three
    gods, as faith in Christ acknowledges in an orthodox way.
    For this does away with offenses, results in a peaceful
    dwelling place: for which the heavenly procession rejoices
    in sweet concord.
    And, clothed in white garments, they follow in the foot-
    steps of the Most High,
    And they wait for the new robes which they desire
    earnestly, over the ages;
    And the grace of God reveals to us what we will add
    over and above our trespasses
    So that the heavenly troop remains united with us af-
    ter burial.

And, the ultimate and highest dividing line passed, we
might be able then to enjoy to the full the palatial dwell-
ings
In which blazes a clear light, lighted by a constant flame,
which vision is God, our eternal salvation,
Who illuminates strongly the hearts of angels so that on
Christ alone they fix firmly their eyes,
For he is the object for which the bodies and souls of the
saints thirst with a parching thirst, along with the per-
petual rewards that will be given them by the judge for
their goodness.

10. Let us sing to the Lord, for he is gloriously triumphant:
horse and rider he has thrown into the sea. The Lord has
become for me my helper and protector unto salvation.

11. Christ having risen from the dead dies now no more:
death shall have no more dominion over him. [For the
life he lives, he lives with God. Alleluia, Alleluia.]

12. From the earth you formed me and with flesh you clothed me:
My Redeemer Lord, raise me up at the Last Day.

13. The Lord our God is worthy to receive glory and honor and
power; because you have created all things, and because of
your will they were and are made. Blessing be to our God
and Lamb who is seated upon the throne.

14. Behold, the Lord will mount upon a swift cloud and Egypt
will be entered, and the idols of Egypt will tremble before
the face of the Lord of hosts.

15. Behold I come, as it is written in the scroll of the book
regarding me, so that I might do your will, my God, for my
spirit rejoices in God my Savior.

16. I who speak Justice, and am mighty to save.

17. And your vestments like those of the treader in the wine
press.

18. Out of Egypt I called my Son; so that he will come to save
his people [Chester: my people].

19. To rejoice, Lord, in your worthiness, we will sing and play
the harp to your excellence.

20. Israel departed from Egypt--the house of Jacob from a foreign people. Alleluia.
Judea was made his sanctuary, Israel his dominion. Alleluia.

21. Let the heavens rejoice with praises, the earth re-echo with joy.
The archangels celebrate the sacred solemnity with glory.
You just ones of the ages and true lights of the world,
We entreat you with heartfelt prayers: hear our prayers of supplication.
You who close heaven or undo its bars with a word,
Free us from all sins by your command, we beseech you.
You, through whom by precept the health and feebleness of all is controlled,
Heal the sick from death, returning us to strength,
So that when Christ will come as judge at the end of time
He will put us in possession of everlasting joys.
To God the Father be glory, and to his only Son,
With the Spirit, the Paraclete, both now and forever,
Amen.

22. Rejoice in the Lord, you just ones: praise from the upright is fitting.

23. Glory to God in the highest, and peace on earth to men of good will.

24. Glory, praise, and honor to you, Christ Redeemer-king; to whom children poured forth fond hosannas.
Glory, praise. . . .
You are the king of Israel and famous Son of David who comes in the name of the Lord, the blessed King.
Glory, praise. . . .
Each angel host lauds you on high with praise, and mortal man and all creation make reply.
Glory, praise. . . .
The people of the Hebrews came to meet you with palms. We come before you with praise, prayer, and hymns.
Glory, praise. . . .

25. Glory to you, Lord.

26. Glory to you, Trinity in unity, one God, before all ages, now and forever.

27. This is the altar of the God of heaven.

28. This is the one who was ignorant of fleshly fault [*LC*, faults]; she will have fruit [*LC*, rest] in the restoring [*LC*, in caring for] of the holy souls.

29. Hosanna to the Son of David. Blessed is he who comes in the name of the Lord. King of Israel [*Chester omits*]. Hosanna in the highest.

30. That one is beautiful among the daughters of Jerusalem, as you see her, full of love and esteem, so that with rejoicing she is taken up to heaven and is seated at the right hand of her son in a throne of glory.

31. That one, beautiful in his robes, walking so full of strength.

32. Jesus, crown of virgins, whom that mother conceived who alone gave birth as a virgin, accept mercifully these prayers.
    You who feed among the lilies surrounded by the dancing of virgins,
    Brides decked with glory and endowed with bridal gifts,
    Wherever you proceed, the virgins follow and, singing,
    dance after you with praises and cry out sweet hymns.
    We pray you to increase your grace to us more abundantly
    so that we may not know at all the wounds of corruption.
    To God the Father be glory, and to his only Son,
    With the Spirit, the Comforter, both now and forever. Amen.

33. Be glad and rejoice in the Lord, you just ones; and glory, all you virtuous of heart.

34. Praise and glory to you.

35. My soul glorifies the Lord, and my spirit rejoices in God my Savior.

36. The sea saw and fled; the river Jordan flowed backward.

37. Fear not, Mary, for you have found favor with the Lord. Behold, you shall conceive and bear a son. Alleluia.

38. Not to us, Lord, not to us but to your name give glory.

39. Now dismiss your servant, Lord, in peace, because my eyes have seen your salvation.

40. My heart is obedient, O God, my heart is obedient. I will sing and utter a psalm to the Lord.

41. Peace be unto you and it will not delay.

42. Who is this one who comes up from the desert rich in allurements, supported by her beloved?

43. Who is this one who comes from Edom, from Bosra, in dyed garments?

44. Lord, Savior of the world, who protected us on this day, Protect us during this night and watch over us at all times.
Come now propitiously and spare your suppliants.
Blot out our offenses, lighten the darkness.
Let no sleep burden our spirits nor the Enemy steal us away;
Nor let us be attacked by any evil that might sully us.
We entreat you, reviver of our senses, with heartfelt prayers
So that we might rise from our beds with pure spirits.
To God the Father and his only-begotten Son be glory,
With the Spirit Paraclete, now and forever. Amen.

45. Holy, holy, holy; Lord God of hosts.

46. The just and devout Simeon waited for the redemption of Israel, and the Holy Spirit was in him.

47. The star of heaven, who nursed the Lord, uprooted the plague of death that was planted by the first ancestor of man.
This same star now is worthy to restrain the stars whose wars slaughter people with the horrible wound of death.
O glorious star of the sea, hear us: from this plague rescue us; for your Son, denying you nothing, honors you.
Save us, Jesus, we for whom your virgin mother prays to you.

48. Rise up, my dearest one, my dove, tabernacle of glory, container of life, heavenly temple.

49. We praise you, O God; we acknowledge you the Lord.
All the earth worships you, the Father everlasting.
To you all angels, the heaven, and the powers of the universe cry out unceasingly:

Holy, holy, holy, Lord God of hosts;
Heaven and earth are full of the majesty of your glory.
The glorious company of the Apostles, the praiseworthy
fellowship of the Prophets, the white-robed throng of
Martyrs all praise you.
The holy Church throughout the whole world acknowledges
you,
The Father of infinite majesty; your worshipful, true,
and only Son; and the Holy Spirit, the Comforter.
You, O Christ, are the King of Glory.
You are the Father's everlasting Son.
When you undertook to free man you did not shrink from
the womb of the Virgin.
When you overcame the sting of Death, you opened to be-
lievers the kingdom of heaven.
You sit at the right hand of God, in the glory of the
Father.
We believe that you will come to judge the world.
We beseech you, therefore, help your servants whom you
redeemed with your precious blood.
Make them to be counted among your saints in eternal
glory.
Save your people, Lord, and bless your heritage.
And govern them and uphold them forever.
Day by day we bless you, and praise your name forever,
world without end.
Be pleased, O Lord, to keep us without sin.
Have mercy on us, O Lord, have mercy on us.
Let your mercy be upon us, O Lord, we who put our trust
in you.
In you, O Lord, I have trusted: let me never be confounded.

49a. To you all angels, the heaven, and the powers of the universe cry out unceasingly: Holy, holy, holy, Lord God of
hosts.

50. I trod the winepress alone, and not one man of courage
came with me from the people.

51. Come Holy Spirit, Creator, visit the souls of your own.
Fill the hearts, which you have created, with celestial
grace.
You, named the Paraclete, gift of God most high,
Living fountain, fire, love, and anointing of the spirit;
You are sevenfold in grace, finger of God's right hand;
You who rightly are the promise of the Father, enriching
throats with speech:

Inflame our senses with light, pour love into our hearts;
Strengthen the weakness of our bodies with your power
forever;
Drive our foes far off and give peace continuously;
Guide us so that by your leading the way we avoid all
harm.
Through you let us know the Father and the Son,
You, the Spirit of both of them, in whom we believe for
all time.
Praise to the Father with the Son, together with the Holy
Paraclete:
And the Son sends us the gift of the Holy Spirit. Amen.

52. Come from Lebanon, my bride; come so that you may be
crowned.

53. Come [LC adds thou] my chosen one, and I will place you
on my throne because the king greatly desires your beauty.

54. Come you blessed ones of my father: receive the kingdom
that was prepared for you from the beginning of the world.

55. Men of Galilee, why are you looking up into the heavens?
This Jesus who was taken up from you into the heavens will
come again in the same way.
Alleluia.

1. King David and musicians. Glasgow, Hunterian Museum Library, MS. 229, fol. 21ᵛ.

2. Musicians playing a transverse flute, nakers, and a bagpipe. Oxford, Bodleian Library, MS. Bodley 264, fol. 123[r].

3. Musicians playing a tabor and flute, a psaltery, a fiddle,
and a long trumpet. Oxford, Bodleian Library, MS. Ashmole
1523, fol. 99[r].

5. Huntsman blowing a horn. Oxford, Bodleian Library, MS. Douce 219-20, fol. 49r.

4. Angels playing a fiddle and portative organ. Oxford, Bodleian Libary, MS. Douce 144, fol. 23r.

6. Angels with horns. Oxford, Bodleian Library, MS. Douce 180, p. 23.

APPENDIX   2

LITURGICAL MUSIC SOURCES

1.   Accipite spiritum sanctum   AS, 280

2.   Adiutorium nostrum

3.   Alma Chorus   Sarum Gradual, BL MS.
                                         Add. 12194, fol. 121^V;
                                         Sarum Breviary, Bodl.
                                         MS. E Mus. 2, p. 379

4.   Ascendo ad Patrem   AS, 270

5.   Assumpta es Maria   GS, 195; AS, 499

6.   Ave Maria . . . sesena   Sarum Gradual, BL MS.
                                         Add. 12194, fol. 126^V

7.   Ave regina celorum   AS, 529

8.   Beatam me dicent   AS, 498

9.   Benedicta sit beata Trinitas   Sarum Gradual, BL MS.
                                         Harl. 622, fol. 126^V

10. Cantemus Domino   (*Liber Usualis*, pp.
                                         649-50)

11. Christus resurgens   GS, 121; AS, 241

12. De terra plasmati me   York Manual, 100

13. Dignus es domine   GS, 82; AS, 256

14. Ecce dominus ascendet

15. Ecce venio

16. Ego qui loquor

17. Et vestimenta tua

18. Ex Egipto vocavi   AS, 20, 21

19. Exaltare domine   AS, 271; AS, 274

20. Exiit Israel

21. Exultet celum   AS, plate Q

22. Gaudete justi   GS, 218; AS, plate K

23. Gloria in excelsis Deo   AS, 53; AS, 47

24. Gloria laus et honor   GS, 83

25. Gloria tibi Domine   AS, 84

26. Gloria tibi Trinitas   AS, 286

27. Hec est ara Dei caeli

28. Hec est que nescivit   AS, 666

29. Hosanna filio David   AS, 206

30. Ista est speciosa

31. Iste formosus

32. Jesu corona virginum   Collectar with Hymns,
                                        BL MS. Harl. 2961, fol.
                                        250[r]

33. Laetamini in Domino   Sarum Gradual, BL MS.
                                        Harl. 622, fol. 217[r]

34. Laus tibi cum gloria

35. Magnificat anima mea   (*Liber Usualis*, pp.
                                        207-18)

36. Mare vidit

37. Ne timeas Maria

38. Non nobis Domine

39. Nunc dimittis   GS, plate k; AS, 404
(*Liber Usualis*, p. 271, etc.)

40. Paratum cor meum   AS, 117

41. Pax vobis

42. Que est ista

43. Quis est iste

44. Salvator mundi   AS, 46

45. Sanctus

46. Simeon justus   AS, 403; AS, 400

47. Stella celi   Cambridge University
Library MS. Add. 6668, fols. 112^r-112^v

48. Surge proxima mea

49. Te Deum   (*Liber Usualis*, pp. 1832-37)

50. Torcular calcavi solus

51. Veni creator spiritus   Sarum Breviary, BL MS. E Mus. 2, fol. 378^r

52. Veni de libano

53. Veni electa mea   GS, 227; AS, 666; YB, fols. 48^v, 144^r, 53^r

54. Venite benedicti   GS, 120; AS, 158

55. Viri galilei, quid aspicitis   AS, 269

APPENDIX 3

Subject	Chester	Coventry	Ludus Cov.	Norwich	Towneley	York
Creation & Fall	Minstrels (6) Dignus es dei Gloria tibi unnamed		Te Deum			Te Deum Te Deum
Noah	Save me Pottell of Malmesey		Mare vidit Non nobis unnamed			unnamed
Prophets						
Pharoah					Harp	Cantemus
Mary's birth & childhood			Benedicta sit (2) Adjutorium Exultet celum Jesu corona Alma chorus Veni creator unnamed (2)			
Annunciation & Visitation	Magnificat		Ave Maria Ave regina	Wythe dolorous With Hart Music		Magnificat Ne timeas unnamed
Trial of Mary & Joseph			unnamed			

Subject	Chester	Coventry	Ludus Cov.	Norwich	Towneley	York
Nativity & Shepherds	Gloria Troly loly Horn (2) Hec est ara unnamed (2)	Gloria (2) Lully As I out rode	Gloria Stella coeli		Gloria (2) unnamed (6) lullay	Gloria unnamed(3)
Magi	minstrels	minstrels	minstrel			
Innocents	Ecce dominus Ex egipto		minstrel		unnamed	
Herod			minstrel			
Purification	Nunc dimittis	Bells Rejoyce Beholde unnamed(3)	Nunc dimittis		Simeon justus bells	
Christ in the Temple	minstrels					
Christ's ministry	Hosanna		Gloria tibi Gloria laus			Hosanna Veni creator(2) unnamed
Harrowing	Te Deum unnamed				Te Deum Salvator mundi	Laus tibi unnamed(2)

Subject	Chester	Coventry	Ludus Cov.	Norwich	Towneley	York
Resurrection	Christus resurgens				Christus resurgens	Christus resurgens
Ascension	Ascendo ad patrem Quis est iste Iste formosus Ego qui loquor Et vestimenta Torculor calcavi Exaltare domine Viri galilei		unnamed		Ascendo	Ascendo
Pentecost	Veni creator Accipite					Veni creator
Thomas of India					Pax vobis(2)	

Subject	Chester	Coventry	Ludus Cov.	Norwich	Towneley	York

Death, Appearance & Assumption of Mary			instrumental (2)
			unnamed (3)
			Veni electa
			Paratum cor
			Hec est que
			Beatam me
			Veni de libano
			Que est ista
			Ista est
			    speciosa
			Exiit israel
			Assumpta es
			Ecce venio
			De terra
						Ave Regina
						Veni electa
						Veni de
						    libano
						Surge
						unnamed (2)

Antichrist	Gaudete					
Judgement	Venite Laetamini (or Salvator) Horn				Te Deum Horn	unnamed (2) Horn

APPENDIX 4

The Chester Plays: A Concordance of Deimling-Matthews
    with Lumiansky-Mills

Deimling-Matthews	*Lumiansky-Mills*
p. 5, lines 99-103	omitted
6, lines 115-18	omitted
8, lines 178-88	omitted
12, lines 61-64	p. 4, lines 82-85
13, lines 101-04	6, lines 121-25
16, after line 192	9, after 213
18, lines 225-28	11, lines 246-49
20, preceding line 1	13, preceding line 1
24, after line 112	17, after line 112
31, after line 280	25, after line 280
36, after line 384	29, after line 384
37, after line 424	31, after line 424
44, after line 616	38, after line 616
57, lines 225-32	52, lines 225-36
58, after line 257	53, after line 252
78, line 350	72, line 350
107, after line 64 and ff.	100, after line 64 and ff.
130, after lines 680-84	122, after lines 666-70
134, lines 45-48 and ff.	126, lines 45-48 and ff.
139, lines 169-72 and ff.	132, lines 161-64 and ff.
141, line 216	134, line 205
147, after lines 368-460	141, after lines 357-449
152, lines 483-90	146, lines 472-79
157, after line 606, lines 29-36	153, lines 625-32

p. 158, lines 617-22   p. 154, lines 651-56

159, line 657, note   156, line 691

166, after line 144   162, after line 144

196, after line 264   194, after line 264

205, lines 493-96 and ff.   204, lines 494-97 and ff.

211, lines 165-68 and ff.   210, lines 163-66 and ff.

257, lines 205-08 and ff.   259, lines 205-08 and ff.

322, line 118   330, line 126

326, lines 193-96   334, lines 209-12

329, lines 259-60 and ff.   337, lines 275-76 and ff.

330, line 283   337, line 299

337, after line 153   345, after line 153

367, after line 104   373, after line 104

369, after line 152   376, after line 152

376, after line 120   383, after line 120

381, after line 238   388, after line 238

426, line 702   436, line 694

427, after line 730   438, after line 722

428, lines 33-40 and ff.   439, lines 33-40 and ff.

429, line 46   440, line 46

445, after line 508   456, after line 508

NOTES

Chapter I. Introduction

[1]See Elisabeth Beuscher, *Die Gesangseinlagen in den englischen Mysterien* (Münster: Helios-Verlag, 1930); Fletcher
Collins, Jr., "Music in the Craft Cycles," *PMLA*, 47 (1932),
613-21; R. W. Ingram, "The Use of Music in the English Miracle
Plays," *Anglia*, 75 (1957), 55-76; John Stevens, "Music in
Medieval Drama," *Proceedings of the Royal Musical Association*,
84 (1957-58), 81-95; Nan Cooke Carpenter, "Music in the Chester
Plays," *Papers on English Language and Literature*, 1 (1965),
195-216, and "Music in the English Mystery Plays," in *Music in
English Renaissance Drama*, ed. John H. Long (Lexington: Univ.
of Kentucky Press, 1968), pp. 1-31. Richard Rastall, in his
forthcoming essay on the music in the Chester cycle to be included in the second volume of the Lumiansky and Mills edition
of the plays for EETS, discusses functions of music, evidence
for music, and possible performance.

[2]Ingram, pp. 55-56, 74. See also E. D. Mackerness, *A
Social History of English Music* (Toronto: Routledge and Paul,
1954), p. 27, and M. L. Spencer, *Corpus Christi Pageants in
England* (New York: Baker and Taylor, 1911), pp. 196-201.

[3]The work in its entirety is contained in my 1972 dissertation for the Center for Medieval Studies, University of
Toronto, and in part in two articles, "Music and the English
Mystery Plays," *Comparative Drama*, 7 (1973), 135-49, and "Mysteries, Minstrels, and Music," *Comparative Drama*, 8 (1974),
112-24 (rpt. under title *Studies in Medieval Drama in Honor of
William L. Smoldon*, 1974 [reissued, Kalamazoo: Medieval
Institute Publications, 1979]). For the dissertation, I studied
the manuscripts of the four complete cycles and the single plays
that may have been part of cycles now lost as well as corporation records and papers of the guilds that produced the plays,
restricting the documents to those from towns with surviving
play texts, so that the records and plays would illuminate one
another. To test the theory that the *Ludus Coventriae* Cycle
was performed at Lincoln (see Hardin Craig, *English Religious
Drama of the Middle Ages* [Oxford: Clarendon Press, 1955],

pp. 265-80, and Kenneth Cameron and Stanley J. Kahrl, "The N-Town Plays at Lincoln," *Theatre Notebook*, 20 [1965-66], 61-69, I examined that city's guild, municipal, and cathedral manuscripts, but I found scanty information about music in the plays produced there and no confirmation from the references to music of links between the cycle and Lincoln. External evidence regarding the performance of the Towneley plays is of a problematical nature (see Jean Forrester and A. C. Cawley, "The Corpus Christi Play of Wakefield: A New Look at the Wakefield Burgess Court Records," *Leeds Studies in English*, n.s. 7 (1974), 108-16), and I found nothing containing further information about that cycle.

The records pertaining to music in the plays were transcribed and collected together in the dissertation; since that time, Records of Early English Drama has begun to publish documents dealing with drama, music, and ceremony and will, as a result, include these particular extracts. I am grateful to Lawrence Clopper and R. W. Ingram for allowing me to check my transcriptions against theirs in the latter's forthcoming REED volume *Coventry* and the former's *Chester* (Records of Early English Drama, 1979), while it was still in proof.

[4] Chester City Record Office, Accounts of the Guild of Painters, 1567-90, unfoliated [fols. 35^r-59^v *passim*].

[5] British Library MS. Harl. 2054, fols. 15^r-21^r; Chester, 211.after 168. All citations in this chapter to plays will be from the editions listed in the Preface and will be indicated by line and page references in the text.

[6] Chester City Record Office, Accounts of the Company of Cordwainers, 1547-98 [modern foliation, fols. 16^r, 16^v].

[7] The Precentor: Harl. 2054, fol. 17^r; Accounts of the Dean and Chapter of Chester Cathedral, vol. 1, p. 97. The Organist: Harl. 2054, fol. 18^v; Accounts of the Dean and Chapter, vol. 2, pp. 50 and 65; J. C. Bridge, "The Chester Miracle Plays. . . ," *Journal of the Architectural, Archaeological, and Historical Society of Chester and North Wales*, 9 (1903), 96.

[8] Weavers' Account Book, fol. 36^v et *passim*; Drapers' Account Book, fol. 39^r et *passim*.

[9] Harl. 2054, fol. 19^v.

[10] Smiths: Thomas Sharp, *A Dissertation on the pageants . . . at Coventry* (Coventry, 1825), pp. 35ff and 207-18; J. O.

Halliwell-Phillips, *Outlines of the Life of Shakespeare*, 4th ed (London: Longmans Green, 1884), pp. 383ff. Drapers: Account Book, fol. 58^r *et passim*. Cappers: Coventry Fellowship of Cappers and Feltmakers, Account Book, 1495-1584, fol. 48^r *et passim*. Weavers: Account Book, fol. 43^r *et passim*.

[11]Sharp, *Dissertation*, p. 213.

[12]Hewett is first named in the account of 1554 (Coventry Corporation MS. A11, Weavers' Account Book, fol. 43^r), and is paid regularly until 1579, the last account for the pageant. He was a wait of Coventry by 1562, when he was paid for his par of the waits' liveries (MS. A7, Chamberlains' Accounts, p. 254) and was still in the city's employ in 1584 (MS. A7, Wardens' Accounts, p. 108). His name is written after the second song, "Beholde now it is come to pass," at the end of the Weavers' play (fol. 17^v). Thomas Nicolls, a wait in 1562 (Chamberlains' Accounts, p. 262), was paid by the Drapers for "settynge a songe" in 1566 (Drapers' Accounts, p. 65) and by the Cappers for "prikinge þe songes" in 1569 (Sharp, *Dissertation*, p. 48).

[13]"Sr. Stephyn Prowet" was paid by the Grocers in 1534 "for makyng of a newe ballet" (Norfolk Record Office, MS. 21(f) 11, no. 68. Robert Fitch in "Norwich Pageants, The Grocers' Play," *Norfolk Archaeology*, 5 (1859), 24, notes that "Sir Stephen Prewett was Seventh Prebend of the College of St. Mary in the Fields in 1536, and one of the Stipendiary Priests of St. Peter Mancroft Church." Waterhouse (*The Non-Cycle Mystery Plays*, EETS, e.s. 104 [1909], p. xxviii) finds in the Church-warden's Accounts of St. Mary's Bungay, Suffolk, "payments in 1526 for copying the game book, *and to Stephen Prewett for his labour in the matter*." This repeats the statement of L. G. Bolingbroke, "Pre-Elisabethan Plays and Players in Norfolk," *Norfolk Archaeology*, 11 (1892), 338: "in 1526 the Churchwarden paid for the copying out of the game book, 4s., and 'to Ser Prewett prest of Norwic, for his labour & costs, iiij s'." Francis Blomefield, in *An Essay towards a topographical history of the County of Norfolk*, IV (London: Wm. Miller, 1806), 258, states that Prewett was presented as rector of St. Margaret of Westwick in 1544, and as stipendiary priest of St. Peter Mancroft in 1547 (p. 186). In 1556, according to Blomefield (p. 187) "Sir Stepen Prewet or Prowet, then parish chaplain, was in-stituted to the rectory of St. Peter in Mancroft, at the pre-sentation of Barbara Catlyn, widow aforesaid, and was inducted and held it for life." Finally, in a will of 1559, Stephen Prowet, clerk, requests burial at the "entre of the quyer dore of the parisshe churche of Saynt Peters of Mancroft," with the

epitaph, "Jhesu have mercye of the sowle of Sir Steven Prowet ffirst parson of this Church" (Norfolk Record Office, Consistory Court, ref. Goldingham, 1559-60, fols. 314^r-318v).

[14]Stevens, "Music in Medieval Drama," pp. 83, 87.

[15]Carpenter, "Music in the English Mystery Plays," p. 25.

[16]Although Wardens' Accounts for the years preceding 1574 are not extant, the regularity of the amounts given after that year and by the Chamberlains for the thirty years their accounts pre-date those of the Wardens lead one to suppose that the sums were constant for this period. Quarterage was also collected by the waits, but at the mid-fifteenth century rate of one penny from every hall and one-half penny from every cottage (Leet Book, fol. 18^r; Mary Dormer Harris, *The Coventry Leet Book*, I, EETS, o.s. 134 [1907], p. 59) the yearly wages of the waits would not have been significantly increased (cf. VCH: *A History of the County of Warwick*, VIII, ed. W. B. Stephens [London, 1969], 4-5).

[17]Coventry Leet Book, fol. 99^r; Harris, p. 189.

[18]Beverley Corporation Documents, Great Gild Book, fols. 41^v-42^r (1555); York Corporation MSS., Memorandum Book B/Y, fols. 222^r-223^v (1561), and Register of Miscellaneous Deeds, fols. 142^r-143^r (1578).

[19]Governors' Minute Book, fols. 184^r, 205^r, and 230^v; Account roll of 1502/3.

[20]Mayors' Court Book IX, p. 682.

[21]House Book 23, fol. 40^r.

[22]Nan Cooke Carpenter, "Music in the *Secunda Pastorum*," *Speculum*, 26 (1951), 697.

[23]Below, p. 138, fn. 23.

[24]J. Wickham Legg, ed., *The Sarum Missal* (Oxford: Clarendon Press, 1916), pp. 428, 447; A. Jefferies Collins, ed., *Manuale ad usum . . . Sarisburiensis*, Publications of the Henry Bradshaw Society, 91 (1958), p. 158.

[25]See, for example, Chester, 20.beginning of the play and n.; Towneley, 116.502; Chester, 197.after 288; York, 505.after

216; Ludus Coventriae, 366.315-19.

[26]For example, the Chester Banns call for music in the Smiths' play (p. 6, lines 115-18), but the text gives no indication of what is performed or where in the action it occurs. At the other extreme is the York "Ne timeas Maria" which seems superfluous to the text as given in the manuscript, since it is sung by the angel only eight lines after he has already greeted Mary with another song.

Moreover, ambiguities in the manuscripts can be carried over into editions which, failing to clarify the problems, misrepresent even further. Miss Carpenter refers in both her articles on music in the cycles to the "'fluryshe' [of trumpets] indicated as 'Balacke Rex' enters and introduces himself as 'Kinge of Mobe land'" ("Music in the Chester Plays," p. 198, and see also "Music in the English Mystery Plays," p. 19). The manuscript, however, clearly shows that the flourish (Chester, 88.fn. for line 105) refers not to the musical announcement of royalty but to the gesture Balaack is to make with the sword mentioned marginally on the same folio of the manuscript (W, fol. 31^r). The directions, all marginal, are "fluryshe," "sworde," and "cast up"; the word "fluryshe" is written, not at Balaack's entry, but beside the line "For sworde ne knife may not avayle. . . ."

[27]Ludus Coventriae, 68.after 146, 80.after 227, 81.after 259, 366.after 319, 367.after 342, 373.500.

[28]Carpenter, "Music in the Secunda Pastorum," p. 698 and fn. 9, discusses the technical terms in these plays.

[29]Stevens, "Music in Medieval Drama," p. 85, fn. 16a.

[30]John P. Cutts, La Musique de scène de la troupe de Shakespeare (Paris: Éditions du Centre National de la Recherche Scientifique, 1959), p. xxi.

[31]See below, p. 151, fn. 37.

[32]J. R. Moore, "The Tradition of Angelic Singing in English Drama," Journal of English and Germanic Philology, 22 (1923), 90.

[33]The Ancient Cornish Drama, ed. Edwin Norris (Oxford, 1859), I, 43, and II, 177-79; Towneley, 384.587-40.

[34]In the early morality plays, for example, music is per-

formed only by the evil characters, never by the good. See John
Stevens, *Music and Poetry in the Early Tudor Court* (London:
Methuen, 1961), pp. 252-59.

[35] "The Role of Musical Instruments in Medieval Sacred
Drama," *Musical Quarterly*, 45 (1950), 67-84.

[36] Carpenter, "Music in the Chester Plays," pp. 211-13;
"Music in the English Mystery Plays," pp. 28-29.

[37] Bowles, pp. 75-83.

[38] Edgar de Bruyne, *Etudes d'esthétique médiéval* (Bruges:
De Tempel, 1946), II, 108-32; III, 227-38.

[39] M. D. Anderson, *Drama and Imagery in English Medieval
Churches* (Cambridge: Cambridge Univ. Press, 1963), discusses
various art forms--wall-paintings, alabaster carvings, roof
bosses, etc.--which may have received their designs from vernacular literature, including drama. The influence could, of
course, have worked both ways in the passing of time. See also
Yvonne Rokseth, "Une source peu étudiée d'iconographie musicale,"
Revue de musicologie, 14 (1933), 74-85.

[40] "Wythe dolorous sorrowe" and "Rejoyce, rejoyce" (see
Index of Songs, below). The York Fall of Man ends with lines
curiously similar to those in the Norwich play. Just before
Adam and Eve sing "Wythe dolorous sorrowe," Eve says, "Therfor
ower handes we may wrynge with most dullfull song." In the
York version, Adam's last lines are, "Allas! for sorowe and
care!/ owre handis may we wryng" (28.175-76). Perhaps, to conclude the play, he and Eve then sing a vernacular song like
that from Norwich.

[41] See, for example, Chester, p. 107, where the "Magnificat"
is paraphrased, and pp. 367-70, where the whole Ascension sequence of songs is translated and paraphrased.

[42] Phillip's *Patient Grissel* (ed. Greg and McKerrow, Malone
Society Reprints, Chiswick Press, 1909) has directions for three
songs to be sung "to the tune of Damon & Pithias" (line 494), "to
the tune of malkin" (line 839), and "to the tune of the latter
Almain" (line 968). The last reference could be, of course, to
the previous song, that "to the tune of malkin," which happened
to be an allemand in style. The play is dated about 1566
(F.P. Wilson and G. K. Hunter, *The English Drama 1485-1585*
[Oxford: Oxford Univ. Press, 1969], p. 223).

[43]Johannes Wolf, "Anonymi cujusdam Codex Basiliensis," *Vierteljahrsschrift für Musikwissenschaft*, 9 (1893), 409.

[44]Walter L. Woodfill, *Musicians in English Society* (Princeton: Princeton Univ. Press, 1963; rpt. New York, 1969), pp. 201-45.

[45]As well, in York, in the decade preceding the incorporation of the minstrels guild, approximately twelve freemen-minstrels resided in York; see Francis Collins, ed., *Register of the Freemen of the City of York*, 2 vols., Publications of the Surtees Society, 96 (1896), 102 (1899). Of these, the following eight undoubtedly were responsible for the first performance of the Minstrels' play in 1562 (York Corporation MSS., House Book 23, fol. 50^r): Ambrose Burgh, harper (Collins, 2, 3) and searcher of the guild in 1579 (House Book 27, fol. 160^v); Robert Hewet, searcher (1565) and master (1579) of the guild (Chamberlains' Book, C5, p. 155; Misc. Register E22, fol. 142^r), wait (House Books 24, fol. 70^v, and 27, fol. 262^r); Arthur Hodgeson, minstrel (Collins, 2, 4), searcher (1565) of the guild (Chamberlains' Book, C5, p. 155), and wait (House Book 24, fol. 267^r); Robert Husthwait, minstrel (Collins, 1, 279) and wait (House Books 22, fol. 67^v, and 23, fol. 19^r); Thomas Moore, minstrel (Collins, 1, 279) and wait (House Book 23, fol. 19^r); Robert Sparke, minstrel (Collins, 1, 274); Cuthbert Wharton, minstrel (Collins, 1, 274) and searcher (1579) of the guild (House Book 27, fol. 160^v); Nicholas Wright, minstrel (Collins, 1, 266) and wait (House Book 23, fol. 19^r).

Chapter III. Commentary on Index of Songs

[1]Joseph C. Bridge includes a transcription in his article, "Three Chester Whitsun Plays," *Journal of the Architectural, Archaeological, and Historical Society of Chester and North Wales*, 14 (1908), ii.

[2]W. W. Greg, *Bibliographical and Textual Problems of the English Miracle Cycles* (London: A. Moring, 1914), p. 37.

[3]F. M. Salter, "The Trial and Flagellation: A New Manuscript," in *The Trial and Flagellation*, ed. W. W. Greg, pp. 1-73, esp. 43-44n.

[4]Chester, 150.427, 431, and 437.

[5] *AS*, Pl. 53; *Index of Gregorian Chant*, ed. John R. Bryden and David G. Hughes (Cambridge: Harvard Univ. Press, 1969), and Detlev Bosse, *Untersuchung einstimmiger mittelalterlicher Melodien zum "Gloria in excelsis Deo"* (Regensburg: G. Bosse, 1955).

[6] Three of the songs are edited by William Cummings in Lucy Toulmin Smith's *York Plays*, pp. 517-21; cf. also Plates I (Frontispiece), II, III; all six are edited by Ruth Steiner in Sister Catherine Wall, "A Study of 'The Appearance of Our Lady to Thomas'" (unpublished doctoral dissertation, Catholic University of America, 1965), pp. 149, 151, 154, 157-59. These latter transcriptions are not accurate as Miss Steiner relied on Smith's incorrect table of coloration. Miss Steiner's transcriptions are included in an article by Carolyn Wall, "York Pageant XLVI and its Music (with A Note on the Transcriptions by Ruth Steiner)," *Speculum*, 46 (1971), 689-712; even in this more recent edition, they do not appear to have been based on the manuscript. Transcriptions of the songs and a commentary will form part of the forthcoming edition of the York Plays. Through the courtesy of the late Professor Arthur Brown, the then editor, I was able to inspect these transcriptions done by Professor John Stevens.

[7] York Minster Library MS., Breviary of the York Use, fols. 197^v, 200^v, 297^r; *AS*, Pls. 490, 520, 666; *GS*, Pl. 227.

[8] Stevens, "Music in Medieval Drama," p. 94. The date of 1430-40 is given by Lucy T. Smith, *York Plays*, p. xviii, and E. K. Chambers, *The Mediaeval Stage*, II (Oxford: Oxford Univ. Press, 1903), 409. But in *English Literature at the Close of the Middle Ages*, Oxford History of English Literature, II, Pt 2 (Oxford: Oxford Univ. Press, 1947), p. 28, Chambers has revised the date of the manuscript to 1475, presumably on the basis of the conclusions of W. W. Greg, *Bibliographical and Textual Problems*, p. 28 and fn. 1, and the date given the manuscript by the British Library (*Catalogue of Additions to the Manuscripts in the British Museum in the Years 1894-1899* [London, 1901], p. 238). See also Wall, "York Pageant XLVI," p. 694.

[9] See Catherine K. Miller, "The Early English Carol," *Renaissance News*, 3 (1950), 61-64, and Manfred Bukofzer, *Studies in Medieval and Renaissance Music* (New York: W. W. Norton, 1950), 148-69.

[10] Thomas Sharp, *A Dissertation*, p. 113.

[11] For previous editions of the songs, see Index of Songs

above, English Songs No. 1 and No. 4.

[12]R. L. Greene, *Early English Carols*, 2nd ed. (Oxford: Clarendon Press, 1977), p. 368.

[13]Greene, p. 359. See John Stevens, *Music at the Court of Henry VIII*, 2nd ed., Musica Britannica, 18 (London, 1969), Nos. 96, 102-05, and 109 for other examples of carols whose settings do not utilize the carol structure.

[14]Percy Dearmer *et al.*, eds., *The Oxford Book of Carols*, 1st ed. (London: Oxford Univ. Press, 1928), pp. 46-47; Rossell Hope Robbins, ed., *Early English Carols* (New York: Columbia University Press, 1961), 74-76. An exception is R. Rastall, ed., *Two Coventry Carols* (Westleigh, Devon: Antico, 1973).

[15]Bars 21 and 22: Treble, stanzas 1 and 2, under d"; bass, stanzas 2 and 3, under B.

[16]P. xxiv. The *signum* is seen in numbers 2, 13, 14, 15, etc., and the suggestions as to its meaning on pp. 101ff.

[17]I have presumed that the songs from the York cycle would be drawn from the York rather than from the Sarum Use.

[18]All references to the texts and music of songs are found above where songs are listed by incipits, with their location in the plays, in the liturgy, and in liturgical texts given. Where a particular song is discussed in this commentary and not merely mentioned, a reference to the edition is given in a note.

[19]Frank Ll. Harrison, *Music In Medieval Britain* (London: Routledge and Kegan Paul, 1963), p. 65.

[20]Ibid., p. 65.

[21]Ibid., p. 85; Solange Corbin, *Essai sur la musique religieuse portugaise au moyen age* (Paris: Les belles lettres, collection portugaise, 8, 1952), pp. 374-78; Margaret Bent, "New and Little-known Fragments of English Medieval Polyphony," *Journal of the American Musicological Association*, 21 (1968), 147 and note 15.

[22]See above, Index of Songs, Latin Songs 53 and 23.

[23]*Analecta Hymnica*, ed. Clemens Blume and Guido Dreves, LII

(Leipzig, 1911), 154. The sequence "Benedicta sit beata Trinitas" sung in the same play and in the Conception of Mary was also performed at marriages (*Missale . . . Westmonasteriensis*, ed. J. Wickham Legg, Publications of Henry Bradshaw Society, 12 [London, 1897], col. 1239).

[24] Harrison, *Music in Medieval Britain*, p. 92.

[25] Ten other songs also show this correspondence: "Beatam me" (*Ludus Coventriae* Assumption, feast of the Assumption), "Exaltare Domine" (Chester Ascension, feast of the Ascension), "Gloria in excelsis" (the Nativity plays in all cycles, Christmas), "Hosanna filio David" (York and Chester Entry into Jerusalem, Palm Sunday), "Ne Timeas Maria" (York Annunciation, feast of the Annunciation), "Nunc dimittis" (Chester and *Ludus Coventriae* Purification, feast of the Purification), "Simeon justus" (Towneley Purification, feast of the Purification), "Veni Creator" (Chester and York Descent of the Holy Spirit, feast of Pentecost), "Veni electa mea" (*Ludus Coventriae* Assumption and York Appearance of Our Lady to Thomas, feast of the Assumption), and "Viri Galilei" (Chester Ascension, feast of the Ascension).

"Gloria in excelsis": an angel apparently sings the "Gloria" in the York cycle, since the shepherds discuss it and try to imitate the song, but there is no stage direction (*York*, p. 120).

"Hosanna filio David": Although neither the text nor title of the song is given in the York stage directions on 210.287, fn. 1, and 218.545, fn. 1, the Bedellus, 283.314 and 284.342, reveals what was sung: "Osanna þei sange þe sone of dauid. . . ." That "hosanna" is sung is verified also in Memorandum Book A/Y, fol. 253[V], where the 1415 list and description of the plays includes "viij pueri cum ramis palmarum cantant' Benedictus etc."

"Simeon justus": see also Edwin Clark, "A Restored Reading in the Towneley Purification Play," *Modern Language Notes*, 56 (1941), 358-60.

[26] Karl Young, *The Drama of the Medieval Church*, 2 vols. (Oxford: Clarendon Press, 1933); Ernst Schuler, *Die Musik der Osterfeiern und Passionen des Mittelalters* (Kassel und Basel: Bärenreiter, 1951); and R. B. Donovan, *The Liturgical Drama in Medieval Spain* (Toronto: Pontifical Institute of Mediaeval Studies, 1958) together contain the texts of the majority of extant liturgical plays.

[27]All references to liturgical dramas are to Karl Young's
Drama of the Medieval Church unless otherwise noted. "Ascendo
ad patrem": I, 373; "Christus resurgens": I, 298, 303, etc.;
"Gloria in excelsis": II, 13, 14, 84, etc.; "Gloria laus": I,
520; *Carmina Burana*, ed. Bernhard Bischoff, facs. ed., Publications of Medieval Music, 9 (Brooklyn, 1967), fol. 107^r;
"Hosanna filio David": I, 520 (Young suggests this antiphon is
meant to be sung after the text's "Item Pueri" [*Carmina Burana*,
fol. 107^r], although he adds, "This arrangement is not demon-
strably correct"); "Magnificat": II, 247 and 250; "Ne timeas
Maria": II, 247 and 249; "Veni creator": II, 239; "Gloria
tibi Trinitas" and "Venite benedicti": Schuler, Nos. 224 and
637, pp. 201 and 344; "Te Deum": I, 64; II, 52, 209, 211, etc.

[28]"Accipite spiritum": I, 490; "Assumpta es": II, 256;
"Nunc dimittis": II, 251-55; "Viri Galilei": I, 484, 487, etc.

[29]Young, I, 472-73.

[30]Paul Kretzmann, in *The Liturgical Element in Medieval
Drama*, University of Minnesota Studies in Language and Literature, 14 (Minneapolis, 1916), p. 143, locates these three songs
in the Sarum Processional, yet gives neither *Ceremonies and
Processions of the Cathedral Church of Salisbury*, ed. Christopher
Wordsworth (Cambridge: Cambridge Univ. Press, 1902), nor *Processionale ad usum . . . Sarum*, ed. W. G. Henderson (Leeds:
M'Corquodale, 1882), in his bibliography. Since he has not, apparently, used any manuscript sources for his study, the reason
for his attribution of the songs remains a mystery, for the
antiphons do not appear in either edition of the Sarum Processional.

[31]Orléans, Bibliothèque municipale, MS. 201, pp. 227-29;
Liber Usualis (Tournai, 1947), pp. 1536-37.

[32]A 1520 Breviary from Bruges (*Breviarium ad usum . . .
Brugen*, Paris, 1520) and an office from Mantua (*Officium de
inventione sanguinis DNJC*, Venice, 1617) do not contain these
antiphons.

[33]Emile Roy, *Le Mystère de la Passion en France*, Revue
Bourguignonne, 13 (1903) and 14 (1904).

[34]*Le Mystère de la Passion d'Arnoul Greban*, ed. Gaston
Paris and G. Raynaud (Paris: F. Vieweg, 1878), pp. 433-34,
lines 33114ff.

[35]The Stanzaic Life of Christ, ed. Frances Foster, EETS, o.s. 166 (London, 1926), pp. 297-304.

[36]Chester, 197.after 288; Paris and Raynaud, 96.7470ff; Carmina Burana, fols. 105^v and 106^r; Young, II, 456-57.

[37]Stanzaic Life, 112.after 3324.

[38]Chester, 130.after 680; Le Mystère du vieil testament, ed. J. de Rothschild (Paris: Firmin Didot, 1891), VI, 211-13, lines 49,068-97; ibid., p. lxxv; Le Mystere de l'incarnation et nativité de Notre Sauveur et Rédempteur Jésus-Christ, ed. Pierre le Verdier, Société des bibliophiles normands (Rouen, 1884-86), II, 439.

[39]Jacobus of Voragine, Legenda Aurea (Lyon: J. Siber, 1493), fol. xi, b, col. 2; Jacobi a Voragine, Legenda aurea, ed. Th. Graesse, 2nd ed. (Leipzig, 1850), p. 507; Stanzaic Life, pp. 20-21, lines 618-20. Johannes Vriend, The Blessed Virgin Mary in the Medieval Drama of England (Purmerend: Muusses, 1928), p. 29, suggests that the direction in the Stanzaic Life, "Verba Angeli," implies singing, but I cannot agree that either the word or the context justifies such a translation.

[40]See A. M. Bautier-Regnier, "A Propos des sens de neuma et de nota en Latin médiéval," Revue belge de musicologie, 18 (1964), 1-9.

[41]Ludus Coventriae, 365.290-319. Legenda Aurea, fols. 135^v, col. 2; 136^r, col. 1; 136^v, col. 1. Charles Gayley, Plays of our Forefathers (London: Chatto and Windus, 1908), pp. 326-27; W. W. Greg, The Assumption of the Virgin (Oxford: Clarendon Press, 1915), and K. S. Block, the editor of the Ludus Coventriae, have all noted the reliance of the Assumption Play on the Legenda Aurea. Fenno C. Hoffman, "Source of the Words to the Music of York XLVI," Modern Language Notes, 65 (1950), 236-39, discusses the Legenda Aurea with reference to the York songs.

[42]York Breviary, II, 63, 77, 481; Sarum Breviary, II, 446; AS, 666. The alleluia verse inverts the word order: "ponam te in thronum meum" (Sarum Missal, 380, etc.; GS, 227; York Missal, II, 155).

[43]Sarum Breviary, I, ccccxxvii, AS, 117; II, 445, AS, 666; I, mclxx, and III, 685, AS, 490; III, 785, AS, 520; York Brevi-

ary, II, 490, 476; *YB*, 146[v], 143[r].

[44]Sarum Breviary, II, 202; III, 689; *AS*, 116, 499, 494.

[45]*Ludus Coventriae*, 372.482-86; *LC*, fol. 222[r].

[46]See above, Index of Songs, Latin song No. 48.

[47]York Breviary, II, 490.

[48]Chester, 12.after 64. The antiphon: Sarum Missal, p. 95, *GS*, pl. 82; Sarum Breviary, I, dcccxci, *AS*, 256. The respond: Sarum Breviary, I, dccclxviii and dcccxciii; *AS*, 251.

[49]*Ludus Coventriae*, 66.85-90. A number of blessings are similar, although not identical; see, for example, an episcopal blessing for Trinity Sunday (*The Benedictional of Archbishop Robert of Canterbury*, ed. H. A. Wilson, Henry Bradshaw Society, 24 [1902], p. 23.

[50]*Ludus Coventriae*, 199.after 195; Sarum Manual, p. 38; Sarum Breviary, I, cccxix; I, lxxii; II, 331, etc.

[51]York Breviary, I, 526. The line also occurs as the versicle of "O Beata et benedicta," an antiphon on Trinity Sunday in *AS*, 293, and in the Sarum Breviary, Bodl. MS. E mus. 2, pp. 396ff, and as the burden of a three-part carol, "Gloria tibi Domine qui natus est de virgine," in John Stevens, *Medieval Carols*, 2nd ed., Musica Britannica, 4 (London, 1958), p. 33, No. 33. This latter text is the doxology for a number of Office hymns.

[52]Towneley, 340.after 83; T. fol. 112[v]. The editor of the plays has incorectly included "hec est dies quam fecit dominus" in the song; the MS. gives the line to the Third Apostle, whose speech immediately follows.

[53]York, 449.31-32; Y, fol. 218[r]; Chester, 358.169-70; B, fol. 138[v]; D, fol. 117[r]; H, 105[r]; R, 160[v]; W, 137[r]. Cf. also 363.104; B, fol. 140[r]; D, fol. 119[r]; H, fol. 106[v]; R, fol. 162[v]; W, fol. 137[r]. Towneley, 341.96; T, fol. 112[v].

[54]*Liber Usualis*, p. 1702; see Young, *Drama of the Medieval Church*, I, 475.

[55]York, 478.154-55, and 479.after 194; Y, fols. 232[v] and 233[r]. The direction is straightforward, but there is a textual

problem: four lines of the angels' speeches seem to be missing;
they might have provided some inkling regarding the devil's
participation. Cf. Towneley, 203.264, where Mary is called Em-
press of Hell.

[56]Ludus Coventriae, 122.36. The incipits in the two plays
do not reveal which of the two Marian antiphons, "Ave regina
caelorum, mater regis," or "Ave regina caelorum, ave Domina," is
intended. Because the former is not in the York Missal or
Breviary, "Ave regina . . . ave" would seem to be meant for the
York play.

[57]"Accipite spiritum": Chester, 381.after 238. The direction is "Duo Angeli." "Ascendo ad patrem": Towneley, 361.after
253; two angels speak following the song. York, 463; Y, fol.
224; two angels. "Christus resurgens": Chester, 337.after 153,
where two angels sing; Towneley, 317; T, fol. 105[r], two angels
speak to the women. "Laetamini": Chester, 445.after 508, the
speeches of two angels precede the singing. "Simeon justus":
Towneley, 185.after 132, two angels speak after the song. "Veni
creator": York, 177.after 154, the direction calls for two
angels; 181.91, fn. 1 with two angels speaking at the end of
the play; 468.after 96. A textual problem is associated with
this last "Veni creator" in the York Descent of the Holy Spirit.
The direction, p. 468, is "Angelus tunc cantare," but the
Apostles, commenting on the song, say:

> v Apos. . . . As aungellis in þis place,
> þat sais þus in þer sange.
> i Apos. In þare sigging saide þei þus,
> And tolde þer talis be-twene þem two,
> Veni creator spiritus. . . .
> (pp. 469.131-34, fol. 228[r])

The direction is apparently in error here. "Stella coeli":
Ludus Coventriae, 148.75-77. Three shepherds appear in the
play. "Exaltare" and "Viri Galilei": Chester, 369.after 152,
four angels appear in the play. "Cantemus Domino": York,
91.406, three pueri and Moses would sing here.

[58]"Dignus es": Chester, 12.after 64, probably at least
nine angels. "Gloria tibi": Chester, 16.after 192, nine
angels. "Hec est que": Ludus Coventriae, 365.294-95, twelve
or thirteen Apostles. "Hosanna": Chester, 257.after 208,
eight citizens including two boys; York, 209.264-65, apparently
only children. "Laus tibi": York, 395.408, seven Souls.
"Mare vidit" and "Non nobis": Ludus Coventriae, 43.after 253,
the eight persons of Noah's family. "Salvator mundi": Towneley,

294.after 44, seven Souls. "Te Deum": York, 2.after 24, probably nine angels. Chester 329.after 260, at least nine. Towneley, 305.404, at least four souls. "Veni creator": Chester, 376.after 120, twelve Apostles. Unnamed: Chester, 13. after 104; B and D, omitted; H, fol. 2^r; R and W, omitted; probably at least nine angels: 326.195-96; B, fol. 127^r; D, fol. 107^v; H, fol. 94^r, R, fol. 144^v; W, 123^v; at least six Souls. York, 53.266, fn. 2; Y, fol. 31^r; probably four or eight persons: 218.545, fn. 1; fol. 112^v; at least eight citizens: 394.384, fn. 1; fol. 199^v; seven Souls: 493.80; fol. 243^r; six angels: 496.157-58; fol. 244^v; six angels: 505. after 216; fol. 249^r; three angels: 513.after 380; fol. 251^v; three angels. The latter two songs could be, of course, solo polyphony. *Ludus Coventriae*, 41.after 197; LC, fol. 24^r; probably eight.

[59]*Ludus Coventriae*, 17.after 39, LC, fol. 10^v; 65.after 72, fol. 39^v; 68.after 146, fol. 40^v; 80.after 227, fol. 46^v; 81.after 259, fol. 47^v; 82.115, fol. 48^v; 91.after 301, fol. 55^r; 93.334, fol. 55^v; 108.after 340, fol. 66^r; 122.36, fol. 74^r; 135.after 372, fol. 81^v; 167.after 146, fol. 99^v; 199.after 195, fol. 119^r; 241.after 289, fol. 145^r; 350.after 47, fol. 210^v; 366.315-19, fol. 219^v; 372-467, fol. 222^r; 373.500, 222^v; In York, 374.36, fn. 1 (Y, fol. 194^r), a direction for singing does not indicate the singers.

[60]See Sister Catherine Wall's *A Study of "The Appearance,"* pp. 126-28, and "York Pageant XLVI," p. 691, for comments on the economic status of the York Weavers who produced this play.

[61]K. S. Block discusses the grouping of the Mary plays in her introduction to the edition of the cycle, pp. **xx-xxv**.

[62]York, 209.263-65 and Y, fol. 109^v; Chester, 257.after 208; B, fol. 100^r; D, 83^v; H, fol. 73^r; R, fol. 111^v; W, fol. 94^r.

[63]Sharp, *Dissertation*, pp. 113-18; Craig, *Two Coventry Corpus Christi Plays*, pp. 31-32 and 70-71. Craig does not print the music for the Shearmen and Taylors' songs.

[64]The texts are correctly edited as two songs in Greene, *Early English Carols*, pp. 41-42 and note, pp. 359-60; p. 59 and note, p. 368.

[65]Ibid., pp. 317 and 320.

[66] Greene, p. 42.

[67] Ibid., p. 368.

[68] Coventry Corporation MS., A97, fol. 17^v. The songs are printed in Craig, *Two Coventry Corpus Christi Plays*, pp. 70-71.

[69] Coventry MS. A97, fol. 5^v; Craig, p. 45.

[70] Coventry MS. A98, fol. 8^v, omitted by Craig; fol. 9^r, Craig, 53.636; fol. 9^v, Craig, 54.694; fol. 12^r, Craig, 58.after 805. One complete folio, fol. 10, has been torn out of the MS.; it would have contained Simeon's "Nunc dimittis" and prophecy and Anne's recognition of Christ.

[71] See above, p. 2.

[72] Coventry Corporation MS., Chamberlains' Accounts, p. 262; Chamberlains' and Wardens' Accounts, pp. 86, 108, 118, 195, etc.

[73] Coventry Chamberlains' Accounts, p. 262; Drapers' Accounts, fol. 66, Sharp, p. 48.

[74] Norfolk Record Office, MS. 21f(11), No. 68, and Fitch, "Norwich Pageants. The Grocers' Play," p. 23. See also my forthcoming study of the relationship between this manuscript and Fitch's copy.

[75] MS. 21f(11), No. 68, and Fitch, p. 15.

[76] P. 217.

[77] See above, p. 84.

[78] See above, p. 132, fn. 13.

[79] Harrison, *Music in Medieval Britain,* p. 462; M. R. James, *Catalogue of the Manuscripts in the Library of St. John's College, Cambridge* (Cambridge: Cambridge Univ. Press, 1913), p. 273.

[80] Chester, 58.after 256; B, fol. 24^r, D, fol. 19^v, R, fol. 25^r: "Then they sing . . ."; H, fol. 16^r, "Tunc Noe claudet fenestram Archae et per modicum spatium infra tectum cantent psalmum Save mee o God. . ."; W, fol. 20^r, "then the singe."

[81] This is the 1549 Prayer Book version, in *The Parallel Psalter*, ed. S. R. Driver, 2nd ed. (Oxford: Clarendon Press,

1904), p. 192.

[82]Le Huray, *Music and the Reformation*, pp. 157ff; *Cranmer's First Litany, 1544, and Merbecke's Book of Common Prayer Noted, 1550*, facs. ed., ed. J. Eric Hunt (London: SPCK, 1939).

[83]M. Frost, *English and Scottish Psalm and Hymn Tunes* (London: SPCK, 1953), p. 122; the metrical text is given in a setting by John Mundy, *Songs and Psalmes* (London, 1594).

[84]Frost, p. 122.

[85]F. M. Salter, "The Banns of the Chester Plays," *Review of English Studies*, 15 (1939), 432-57, and 16 (1940), 1-17, 137-48. See especially 15, 436.

[86]Chester, 57.225ff; B, fols. 23^v and 24^r; D, fol. 19^r; H, fol. 15^v; R, fol. 24^v; W, fol. 19^v.

[87]The same type of versification appears here and there in the cycle, testifying to a revision, probably in the latter part of the fifteenth century, which added popular elements to the plays. See Salter, "Banns," *Review of English Studies*, 15, 452, and 16, 15. See also above, p. 109, for additional verification of Professor Salter's theory.

[88]See above, p. 136, fn. 3

[89]Chester, 151.after 458; B, fol. 57^v, "tooly holy holy loo"; D, fol. 46^v, "troly loly loly loo"; H, fol. 43^r; R, fol. 62^v, "troly loly lo"; W, fol. 52^v, "troly loly troly loe."

[90]Chester, 157.after line 606, footnotes; B, fol. 60^v; D, fol. 48^v; H, omitted; R, fol. 65^v; W, fol. 55^v.

[91]See above, p. 2.

[92]John Stevens, *Music at the Court of Henry VIII*, pp. 32, 57, and 95, and John Stevens, *Music and Poetry in the Early Tudor Court*, pp. 401, 413-14, 424-25.

[93]Joseph Ritson, *Ancient Songs and Ballads*, I (London: Payne and Foss, 1829), lxxxiv, fn. ‡, and II, 7; Nan Cooke Carpenter, "Music in the Chester Plays," p. 202, fn. 15. Cf. William Langland, *The Vision of William Concerning Piers the Plowman*, ed. W. W. Skeat, I (Oxford: Clarendon Press, 1886), 202, lines 117-18; 203, lines 108-09 and 122-23; John Skelton,

The Complete Poems, ed. Philip Henderson (London: Dent, 1931), pp. 119, 214; *Hickscorner,* Tudor Fascimile Texts, ed. John S. Farmer (London, 1908), fol. Ci^r.

[94] *Ludus Coventriae,* 129.164; LC, fol. 77^v; Towneley, 130.442; T, fol. 43^r.

[95] Craig, *Two Coventry Plays,* 16.471-74.

[96] Towneley, 270.406 and 271.429; T, fol. 89^r.

[97] "Alas" occurs in the York Pharoah, 75.128, Y, fol. 39^r; and in the Towneley Pharoah, 68.141, T, fol. 22^v. Ffroward's "ylla-hayll" is in Towneley, 240.375; T, fol. 77^v. "Well awaye" is in Chester, 78.350, B, fol. 31^r; D, fol. 25^r; H, fol. 21^v; R, fol. 33^r; W, fol. 26^v; and in *Ludus Coventriae,* 176.245; LC, fol. 104^r; 225.8, fol. 136^r; 374.29, fol. 223^v.

[98] Towneley, 108.265-70, T. fol. 35^v; 113-14.422-31, fol. 37^r; 116.497-502, fol. 38^r; 122.186-89, fol. 40^r; 137.659-64, fol. 45^v; 140.753-54, fol. 46^v. York, 120.after 64, Y, fol. 57^r; 121.84-85, fol. 57^r; 122.130-31, fol. 56^r. Chester, 151.after 458, B, fol. 57^v, D, fol. 46^v, H, fol. 43^r, R, fol. 62^v, W, fol. 52^v; 152.487-88, B, fol. 58^r, D, fol. 47^r, H, fol. 43^r, R, fol. 63^r, W, fol. 53^r; 158.617-18, B, fol. 61^r, D, fol. 49^r, H, fol. 44^v, R, fol. 66^r, W, fol. 56^r.

[99] Towneley, 122.186-89; T, fol. 40^r.

[100] Towneley, 116.501-02; T, fol. 38^r.

[101] Carpenter, "Music in the *Secunda Pastorum,*" p. 698.

[102] See Matthew W. Black, *Elizabethan and Seventeenth-Century Lyrics* (Chicago: Lippincott, 1938), p. 214; Gustave Reese, *Music in the Renaissance,* rev. ed. (New York: W. W. Norton, 1959), p. 769; Ernest Walker, *A History of Music in England,* 3rd ed. (Oxford: Clarendon Press, 1952), p. 45; Sir Jack Westrup, "Song," in *Oxford History of Music,* 2nd ed., ed. H. E. Wooldridge (London: Oxford Univ. Press, 1932), II, 350-51.

[103] Woodfill, *Musicians in English Society,* pp. 14-15.

[104] *Macro Plays,* ed. Mark Eccles, EETS, e.s. 262 (1969), p. 72, lines 2332-36.

Chapter V. Commentary on Index of Instruments

[1]Chester, 20.beginning of the play; B, fol. 7[r]. The others are 24.after 112; B, fol. 8[v]; D, fol. 7[r]; R, fol. 10[v]; W, fol. 6[v]; 31.after 280; B, fol. 10[v]; D, fol. 9[r]; R, fol. 13[v]; W, fol. 9[v]; 36.after 384; B, fol. 12[r], D, fols. 11[r] and 11[v]; R, fol. 15[v]; W, fol. 11[r]; 37.after 424; B, fol. 13[r]; D, fol. 12[r]; R, fol. 16[r]; W, fol. 11[v]; 44.after 616: B, fol. 18[v]; D, fol. 14[v]; R, fol. 19[r]; W, fol. 14[r].

[2]Above, p. 79.

[3]Chester, 166.after 144; B, fol. 64[r]; D, fol. 51[v]; R, fol. 69[v]; W, fol. 59[v].

[4]Chester, 6.118; B, fol. 1[v], where "harpe" has been writte[n] crossed out, and replaced by "flute"; R, fol. 2[v].

[5]*Ludus Coventriae,* 152.19, LC, fol. 92[r]; 174.153, LC, fol. 102[v]; 176.232, LC, fol. 104[r].

[6]Chester, 134.after 48; B, fol. 51[v]; D, fol. 42[r]; H, fol. 38[v]; R, fol. 55[v]; W, fol. 46[v]; 138-39.159-72; B, fol. 53[r]; D, fols. 43[r] and 43[v]; H, fols. 39[v] and 40[r]; R, fol. 57[v]; W, fol. 48[r].

[7]Chester, 18.228; 428.33 and after 40; 429.46: B, fols. 6[r] and 166[v]; D, missing; H, fols. 3[v] and 131[v]; R, fols. 7[v] and 194[v]; W, fols. 4[r] and 162[r]. Towneley, 62.199; 367.3; 368.41-42; 370.89; 375.250; T, fols. 19[v], 122[r], 123[r]. York, 499.63-65; 500.115; Y, fols. 246[v] and 247[v].

Inconsistency in the nomenclature of the instruments playe[d] by the angels in the Chester, Towneley, and York Judgment plays raises the perplexing problem of what, precisely, was used in the mysteries to announce the end of the world.

All three plays agree that the beam sounded Christ's comin[g] but Towneley and York describe it additionally as a horn and a trumpe. Chester and York, further, translate beam by *tuba.* A *tuba* is a straight trumpet or trumpe, but a horn is of another family entirely. Moreover, modern writers seem as uncertain about the beam as medieval scribes. Francis Galpin (*Old Englis[h] Instruments of Music,* 4th ed. [London: Methuen, 1965], p. 137) and Curt Sachs (*Real-Lexicon der Musikinstrumente* [1913; rpt. New York: Dover, 1964], p. 44a) call it a horn, but Sybil Marcuse (*Musical Instruments: A Comprehensive Dictionary* [New York: W. W. Norton, 1964], pp. 51-52) considers it to be a trumpet. Gustav Schad (*Musik und Musikausdrücke in den*

mittelenglischen Literatur [Frankfort: H. Richter, 1911], p.
25) suggests that the beam and trumpet were not the same instrument because they were constructed from different materials:
the beam from horn, wood, or bone, the trumpet from metal.
Frederick M. Padelford, *Old English Musical Terms*, in *Bonner
Beitrage zur Anglistik,* IV (1899), points out the confusion,
but considers the beam to be a trumpet.

If a beam is a trumpet and, accordingly, a *tuba*, it is not
a horn. If it is, on the other hand, a horn, it cannot be a
tuba. The confusion in the play texts would seem to indicate
that the structural difference between horns and trumpets was
not clearly realized, and, as a result, the terms were used
interchangeably.

[8] Towneley, 370.107; T, fol. 123^r.

[9] Coventry, 19.538.

[10] Chester, 157.after 606; B, fol. 60^v; D, fol. 48^v; H,
omitted; R, fol. 65^v; W, fol. 55^v. One of the Coventry shepherds also has a pipe, 11.310.

[11] Towneley, 185.after 102; T, fol. 61^v.

[12] Coventry, 45.366; 52.624; 53.633; Weavers' Play, fols.
5^v and 9^r.

[13] Towneley, 59-60.104-05 and 109-10; T, fols. 18^v and 19^r.

[14] *Ludus Coventriae,* 358.90 and the direction following; LC,
fol. 216^r.

[15] *Ludus Coventriae,* 365.after 285; LC, fol. 219^r; 373.after
493; LC, fol. 222^v.

[16] Hardin Craig, *English Religious Drama*, p. 270.

[17] Above, p. 2.

[18] Chester Corporation MSS., Mayor's Book, 25, 1589-92,
28 May, 33 Eliz. I.

[19] Cheshire County Record Office, Will of William Madock,
7 Sept. 1604.

[20] Coventry Corporation MS., Wardens' Account, p. 8.

[21] York Corporation MS., House Book, 24, fol. 59^v, 4 Dec., 9 Eliz. I.

[22] George A. Stephen, "The Waits of the City of Norwich," *Norfolk Archaeology*, 25 (1935), 66.

[23] Coventry Leet Book, II, 391-93. See also Robert Withington, *English Pageantry* (Cambridge: Harvard Univ. Press, 1918), I, 153-54.

[24] Ibid., II, 590. See also Withington, I, 164.

[25] Quoted in Walter Rye, *Extracts from the Records of the Corporation of Norwich* (Margate: Keble, 1902), but the reference is incorrect. The terms of apprenticing are found in the Norwich City Apprenticeship Indentures, 1548-81, Case 17d, fol. 52^r.

[26] British Library MS. Harl. 2054, fols. 15^r-16^v.

[27] York Corporation MS., Memorandum Book B/Y, fol. 222^r.

[28] At the time of the guild's incorporation, at least fourteen freemen-minstrels resided in York; the play would take a minimum of eight actors.

[29] B.L. MS. Lansdowne 896, fols. 153^r-156^v.

[30] George Ormerod, *History of the County Palatine and the City of Chester*, 2nd ed. (London: Lackington, 1882), I, 36, 644

[31] Judgment: Chester, 428.33ff; Towneley, 368.41-42; York, 499.65; Banquet: *Ludus Coventriae*, 174.153-54.

[32] Although no English collections of early fanfares seem to exist, see *Trompeterfanfaren, Sonaten und Feldstücke*, ed. Georg Schünemann, in *Das Erbe deutscher Musik*, 7 (Kassel, 1937).

[33] Edward Halle, *Henry VIII*, ed. Charles Whibley (London: T. C. and E. C. Jack, 1904), I, 8; also John Stevens, *Music and Poetry in the Early Tudor Court*, p. 238. See also *Sir Gawain and the Green Knight*, ed. J. R. R. Tolkien and E. V. Gordon, 2nd ed., ed. Norman Davis (Oxford: Clarendon Press, 1968), p. 4, lines 116-19.

[34] Chester, 134.after 48; 139.after 172. For this type of music, see Schünemann, *passim*.

[35]Whistle: see above, p. 86.   Pipe: Chester, 157.after
606.

[36]Chester, 6.118.

[37]Morris dances: Galpin, *Old English Instruments of Music,*
p. 111.   The only references to dancing in the cycles is the
unusual dance of the torturers in the *Ludus Coventriae* Crucifixion: the executioners are directed to "leve of and dawncyn
a-bowte þe cros shortly" (297.after 753).   How or what these
men would have danced in such a situation is puzzling, but the
answer may perhaps be found in an English alabaster carving de-
picting the scourging of Christ: one of the three torturers in
the carving wears a rope of bells around his waist (W. L.
Hildburgh, "English Alabaster Carvings as Records of the Medieval Religious Drama," *Archaeologia,* 93 [1949], 81, and Pl.
XVIIb).   Bells were part of the costume of a morris dancer;
would this explain the non-committal entry in the account of the
Chester Coopers of the expenses of their Passion Play: "payde
to hugh gyllam iiis iiiid"(fol. 3[r]ff), when Hugh Gillam, a
tailor, was also a morris dancer of some note, paid by the Corporation for dancing at midsummer in 1564 and subsequent years
(Treasurers' Rolls, 1564-65 to 1578)?   Might not Gillam have
played the role of one of the executioners and performed his
dance in the course of the action?   See also A. P. Rossiter's
note that in "Christ Mocked," the 1503 painting by Grünewald,
one of the onlookers is a man playing the pipe and tabor *(English Drama from Early Times to the Elizabethans* [London:
Hutchinson, 1950], p. 181, fn. 19), and *Matthias Grünewald,
Complete Editie van Zijn Schilderijen,* ed. J.-K. Huysmans
and E. Ruhmer (Zeist: W. de Haan, 1958), Pl. I.   In an apparently non-cyclic play, *The Killing of the Children* in the Digby
MS., three dances are performed by the "virgynes" who also sing
the "Nunc Dimittis" in the play (*The Digby Plays,* ed. F. J.
Furnivall, EETS, e.s. 70 [1896], 2.after 56; 22.after 550;
23.566, and 20.after 484, and *The Digby Plays,* facs. ed.,
introd. Donald C. Baker and J. L. Murphy (Leeds, 1976), fols.
146[v], 155[v], 157[r].

[38]Coventry, 45.366; 52.624; 53.633; Towneley, 184.after 102.

[39]Towneley, 59.104-05, and 60.109-10 and 118.

[40]See above, p. 2, for Hewett; for Bakyn, Norfolk Record
Office, MS. 21(f) 11, No. 68.

[41]*Ludus Coventriae,* 358.after 90; 365.after 285; 373.after

493.

[42]Although organ music of the fifteenth century is lacking in English sources, much survives from the later Tudor period. See, for example, *The Mulliner Book,* ed. Denis Stevens, Musica Britannica, 1 (London, 1962); *Music at the Court of Henry VIII,* ed. John Stevens.

[43]Chester, 20.beginning of the play; 24.after 112; 31.after 280; 36.after 384; 37.after 424; 44.617; 166.after 144; *Ludus Coventriae* 152.19-20; 176.231-32.

[44]For contemporary accounts of music of this sort, see E. J. Dent, "Social Aspects of Music in the Middle Ages," *Oxford History of Music,* Introductory Volume, ed. P. C. Buck (London: Oxford Univ. Press, 1929), p. 203; Edmund Bowles, "Musical Instruments at the Medieval Banquet," *Revue belge de musicologie,* 12 (1958), 41-51. One presumes that much of it was extempore.

[45]Coventry, 19.537-39.

[46]Edmund Bowles, "*Haut* and *Bas*: The Grouping of Musical Instruments in the Middle Ages," *Musica Disciplina,* 8 (1954), 118-19, 129.

Chapter VII. Commentary on Glossary of Musical Terms

[1]Of the 68 English and Latin musical terms found in the cycles, Chester uses 21; *Ludus Coventriae,* 20, Towneley, 40; York, 12. Of the shepherds' plays, the figures are: Chester, 18; *Ludus Coventriae,* 6; Towneley, 31; York, 8.

[2]Chester, 148.395-96; 149-50.415-34.

[3]Salter, "Banns," *Review of English Studies,* 15, 452, and 16, 15.

[4]Towneley, 110.36 and 326; 113.413-19; 409-12.

[5]Towneley, 137.656-60.

[6]Willi Apel, *The Notation of Polyphonic Music,* 5th ed. (Cambridge: Harvard Univ. Press, 1953), pp. 96-100.

[7]Towneley, 137.647.

[8]Towneley, 116.502; 122.186-89. Although the singing "in sight" describes only the shepherds' second song at the end of the play, I have presumed that their first song (108.265-70) is in the same style. Cawley, however, feels (*The Wakefield Pageants*, p. 102, fn. 266) that "Who so can best syng/ Shall haue the begynnyng" means the best singer starts the song off, and Hope Traver ("Relation of Musical Terms," *Modern Language Notes*, 20 [1905], 1-5) believes such a method indicates a round. This may indeed be so, but "begynnyng" could also refer to the first drink from the bottle which the Second Shepherd has just produced. He offers it to the man who sings best, and the First Shepherd, who accepts the challenge with "I shall sett you on warke," receives the reward as his due: "We haue done our parte/ and songyn right weyll,/ I drynk for my parte."

[9]Cawley, *The Wakefield Pageants*, pp. xvii-xxx.

[10]See above, pp. 10-11, for a discussion of the effects of music on good and evil characters in the plays.

SELECTED BIBLIOGRAPHY

I. *PRIMARY SOURCES*

A. *Manuscripts*

Beverley, Municipal Offices
    Corporation of Beverley MSS.:
        Account Rolls, 1386-1520/1
        Gild Book, c. 1409-1589
        Governors' Minute Book, 1436-70
        Town Chartulary, c. 1400-52

Chester, City Record Office
    Corporation of Chester MSS.:
        A/B/1: Assembly Books, 1539-1624
        A/F/1: Assembly Files
        Mayors' Books, 5, 6, and 25
        TAR 1-1 to TAR 1-16: Treasurers' Rolls, 1436-1577
    Guild of Painters
        Accounts and Orders, 1567-1690
    Guild of Cordwainers
        Accounts, 1547-98

Chester, Public Library
    Thomas Hughes MSS: Transcripts of Assembly Books

Chester, Cathedral
    Accounts of the Dean and Chapter, Vols. 1 (1542-59) and
        2 (1561-84)

Chester, Company of Coopers
    Account Book, 1571-1611

Chester County Record Office
    Wills in the Diocesan and Probate Registries

Coventry, Record Office
    Corporation of Coventry MSS.:
        A 3: Leet Book, 1251-1555

A 4 and A 5: Account Books of the Carpenters' Guild,
     c. 1454-1586
A 6: Account Book of the Guild of Corpus Christi and
     St. Nicholas, 1488-1553
A 7: Chamberlains' Accounts, 1498-1574
     Chamberlains and Wardens' Accounts, 1574-90
A 11: Account Book of the Weavers' Guild
A 16: Treasurers' Book of Payments, 1561-1653
A 17, A 18, and A 20: Treasurers' Book of Receipts,
     1561-1681
A 97: Pageant of the Weavers'Guild
A 98: Ordinances of the Cordwainers' Guild, 1577
A 99: Account Book and Orders of the Mercers' Guild,
     1579-1829
A 110: Ordinance Book of the Bakers' Guild, c. 1700
A 128A: Orders and Misc. Papers of the Fullers' Guild,
     1475-1770
Daffern Transcripts: Accounts of the Carpenters' Guild
                      Accounts of the Mercers' Guild
                      Accounts of the Drapers' Guild
                      Accounts of the Smiths' Guild

Coventry, Fellowship of Cappers and Feltmakers
     Account Book, 1495-1584

Lincoln, Record Office
     Corporation of Lincoln MSS.:
          Minute Books, I (1511-41), II (1541-64), III (1565-99)

Lincoln, Cathedral
     Chapter Acts, A.2.36 (1465-78), A.2.37 (1479-96)
     Chapter Accounts, Bj/3/2 to Bj/3/6: Books 2-6 (1480-1577)

Lincoln, Public Library
     MS. 5009: The Cordwainers' Book, 1527-1785

London, British Library
     Add. MSS.: 10,305 -- Chester Plays, (MS. W)
                 12,194 -- Sarum Gradual
                 19,517 -- Chester Antiquities
                 33,852 -- Register of the York Bakers' Guild
                 34,604 -- Accounts of the York Bakers' Guild
                 35,290 -- York Plays
     Harl. MSS.: 622 -- Sarum Gradual
                 2013 -- Chester Plays (MS. R)
                 2054 -- Accounts of the Chester Smiths' Guild
                 2093 -- Chester Antiquities

2124 -- Chester Plays (MS. H)
2150 -- Chester Antiquities
2961 -- Sarum Breviary
6388 -- Coventry Antiquities
6466 -- Extracts from the Papers of the Coventry
Butchers, Tylers, and Pinners
Lansd. MS. 896 -- Beverley Antiquities

Norwich, Norfolk Record Office
Corporation of Norwich MSS.:
Liber Albus: Press D, Case 17, shelf b
Old Free Book: Press D, Case 17, shelf b
Apprenticeship Indentures, 1548-81
Assembly Minute Books, 1492-1510: Press D, Case 16,
shelf c
Assembly Proceedings, 1434-1587: Press D, Case 16,
shelf d
Assembly Rolls, 1364-1512: Press B, Case 8, shelf d
Chamberlains' Accounts, 1384-1589: Press E, Case 18,
shelf a
Mayors' Court Books, 1510-69
Papers of the Guild of St. George: Press B, case i,
shelves e, f, g
Account Rolls, 1420-1547
Miscellaneous Papers
MSS. 4634 and 11,345: Extracts from Miscellaneous MSS.
Mann MSS., vols. 1-13: Norwich and Norfolk Musical
Events, etc.
Kirkpatrick Papers, MS. 21(f), no. 68
MSS. of the Dean and Chapter, Norwich Cathedral
Sacrists' Account Rolls, 1399-1536
Precentors' Account Rolls, c. 1420-1536

Orléans, Bibliothèque municipale
MS. 201: Fleury Playbook

Oxford, Bodleian Library
Bodl. MS. 175 -- Chester Plays (MS. B)
Bodl. MS. e. Mus. 2 -- Sarum Breviary
Sancroft MS. 72 -- Chester Antiquities

San Marino, California, Huntington Library
MS. HM 1 -- Towneley Plays
MS. HM 2 -- Chester Plays (MS. D)

York, Public Library
Corporation of York MSS.:

158

C1-1 to C7-1: Chamberlains' Account Rolls, 1397-1562
C1 to C5: Chamberlains' Account Books, 1446-1585
House Books, Nos. 1-29, 1474-1585
A/Y: Memorandum Book, 1376-1493
B/Y: Memorandum Book, 1371-1596
E-22: Register of Miscellaneous Deeds, etc.
Scriveners' Play

York, Minster Library
    Breviary of the York Use

York, Company of Merchant Adventurers
    Miscellaneous Accounts

B. *Editions*

Baker, Donald C., and J. L. Murphy, introd. *The Digby Plays.*
    Leeds Texts and Monographs: Medieval Drama Facsimiles,
    III. Leeds, 1976.

Benedictines of Solesmes. *The Liber Usualis.* Tournai, 1947.

Bischoff, Bernhard. *Carmina Burana,* facs. ed. Publications
    of Medieval Music Manuscripts, 9. Brooklyn: Institute
    of Medieval Music, 1967.

Block, K. S. ed. *Ludus Coventriae, or the Plaie Called Cor-*
    pus Christi. EETS, e.s. 120. 1922; rpt. 1960.

Blume, Clemens, and Guido M. Dreves. *Analecta Hymnica Medii*
    Aevi. 55 vols. Leipzig, 1886-1922.

Breviarium ad usum . . . Brugen. Paris, 1520.

Cawley, A. C. *The Wakefield Pageants in The Towneley Cycle.*
    Manchester: Manchester Univ. Press, 1958.

Cawley, A. C., and Martin Stevens, introd. *The Towneley Cycle.*
    Leeds Texts and Monographs: Medieval Drama Facsimiles,
    II. Leeds, 1976.

Clopper, Lawrence M. *Chester.* Records of Early English Drama.
    Toronto: Univ. of Toronto Press, 1979.

Collins, A. Jefferies. *Manuale ad usum . . . Sarisburiensis.*
    Publications of the Henry Bradshaw Society, 91. 1958.

Collins, Francis. *Register of the Freemen of the City of York*. Publications of the Surtees Society, 96 (1896), 102 (1899).

Craig, Hardin, ed. *Two Coventry Corpus Christi Plays*, 2nd ed. EETS, e.s. 87. 1957.

Cutts, John P. *La Musique de scène de la troupe de Shakespeare*. Paris: Centre national de la recherche scientifique, 1959.

Davis, Norman, ed. *Non-Cycle Plays and Fragments*. EETS, s.s. 1. 1970.

Dearmer, Percy, *et al. Oxford Book of Carols*. London: Oxford Univ. Press, 1928.

Deimling, Hermann, ed. *The Chester Plays*, Part I. EETS, e.s. 62. 1892; rpt. 1959.

Driver, Samuel R. *The Parallel Psalter*, 2nd ed. Oxford: Clarendon Press, 1904.

Eccles, Mark, ed. *The Macro Plays*. EETS, e.s. 262. 1969.

England, George, and A. Pollard, eds. *The Towneley Plays*. EETS, e.s. 71. 1897; rpt. 1952.

Fitch, Robert. "Norwich Pageants. The Grocers' Play," *Norfolk Archeology*, 5 (1859), 8-31.

Foster, Frances, ed. *Stanzaic Life of Christ*. EETS, o.s. 166. 1926.

Frere, Walter Howard. *Antiphonale Sarisburiense*, facs. ed. Plainsong and Medieval Music Society. London, 1901-05.

_____. *Graduale Sarisburiense*, facs. ed. Plainsong and Medieval Music Society. London, 1894.

Furnivall, F. J., ed. *The Digby Plays*. EETS, e.s. 70. 1896; rpt. 1967.

Greg, Walter W. *The Assumption of the Virgin*. Oxford: Clarendon Press, 1915.

Greene, Richard L. *The Early English Carols*. Oxford: Clarendon Press, 1935; 2nd ed., 1977.

Harris, Mary Dormer, ed. *The Coventry Leet Book*. EETS, o.s. 134 (1907), 135 (1907), 138 (1909), 146 (1913).

Henderson, Walter G. *Manuale et Processionale ad usum Eboracensis*. Publications of the Surtees Society, 63. 1874.

_____. *Missale ad usum Eboracensis*. Publications of the Surtees Society, 59, 60. 1874.

_____. *Pontificale ad usum Eboracensis*. Publications of the Surtees Society, 61. 1873.

_____. *Processionale ad usum Sarum*. Leeds: M'Corquodale, 1882.

Hickscorner, facs. ed. Tudor Facsimile Texts. London, 1908.

Hunt, J. Eric. *Cranmer's First Litany, 1544, and Merbecke's Book of Common Prayer Noted, 1550*, facs. ed. London, 1939.

Huysmans, J.-K., and E. Ruhmer. *Matthias Grünewald, Complete Editie van Zijn Schilderijen*. Zeist: W. de Haan, 1958.

Jacobi a Voragine. *Legenda aurea vulgo historia Lombardica dicta*, 2nd ed., ed. Th. Graesse. Leipzig, 1850.

Jacobus de Voragine. *Legenda Aurea*. Lyon: J. Siber, 1493.

Johnston, Alexandra F., and Margaret Dorrell. *York*. Records of Early English Drama. Toronto: Univ. of Toronto Press, 1979.

Langland, William. *The Vision of William concerning Piers the Plowman*, ed. W. W. Skeat. Vol. 1. Oxford: Clarendon Press, 1886.

Lawley, S. W. *Breviarium ad usum insignis ecclesiae Eboracensis*. Publications of the Surtees Society, 71 (1879) and 75 (1882).

Legg, J. Wickham. *Missale Westmonasteriensis*. Publications of the Henry Bradshaw Society, 12. 1897.

_____. *The Sarum Missal*. Oxford: Clarendon Press, 1916.

Le Verdier, Pierre. *Le Mystère de l'Incarnation et Nativité de*

Notre Sauveur et Rédempteur Jésus-Christ. Rouen: Société des Bibliophiles Normands, 1884-86.

Lumiansky, R. M., and David Mills, eds. *The Chester Mystery Cycle*. EETS, s.s. 3. 1974.

_____, introd. *The Chester Mystery Cycle*. Leeds Texts and Monographs: Medieval Drama Facsimiles, I. Leeds, 1973.

Matthews, Dr., ed. *The Chester Plays*, Part II. EETS, e.s. 115. 1916; rpt. 1959.

Meredith, Peter, and Stanley J. Kahrl, introd. *The N-Town Plays*. Leeds Texts and Monographs: Medieval Drama Facsimiles, IV. Leeds, 1977.

Mundy, John. *Songs and Psalmes*. London, 1594.

Norris, Edwin. *The Ancient Cornish Drama*. 2 vols. Oxford, 1859.

Officium de inventione sanguinis DNJC. Venice, 1617.

Paris, Gaston, and Gaston Raynaud. *Le Mystère de la Passion d'Arnoul Greban*. Paris: F. Vieweg, 1878.

Phillip, John. *The Play of Patient Grissell*, ed. W. W. Greg and R. B. McKerrow. Malone Society Reprints. Chiswick Press, 1909.

Proctor, Francis, and Christopher Wordsworth. *Breviarium ad usum Sarum*. 3 vols. Cambridge: Cambridge Univ. Press, 1879-86.

Rastall, Richard, ed. *Two Coventry Carols*. Westleigh, Devon: Antico, 1973.

Robbins, Rossell Hope. *Early English Christmas Carols*. New York: Columbia Univ. Press, 1961.

Rothschild, Baron James de. *Le Mistère du vieil testament*. 6 vols. Paris: Firmin Didot, 1878-91.

Roy, Emile. *Le Mystère de la Passion en France*. Revue Bourguignonne, 13 (1903), 14 (1904).

Rye, Walter. *Extracts from the Records of the Corporation of Norwich*. Margate: H. Keble, 1902.

Schünemann, Georg. *Trompeterfanfaren, Sonaten und Feldstücke*. Das Erbe deutscher Musik, 7. Kassel, 1937.

Sharp, Thomas. *A Dissertation on the pageants or dramatic mysteries, anciently performed at Coventry*. Coventry, 1825.

_____. *The Presentation in the Temple*. Edinburgh: Abbotsford Club, 1836.

_____. *The Pageant of the Company of Sheremen and Taylors in Coventry*. Coventry, 1817.

Skelton, John. *The Complete Poems*, ed. Philip Henderson. London: Dent, 1931.

Smith, Lucy Toulmin, ed. *York Plays*. 1885; rpt. New York: Russell and Russell, 1963.

Stevens, Denis, ed. *The Mulliner Book*. Musica Britannica, 1. London, 1962.

Stevens, John, ed. *Medieval Carols*, 2nd ed. Musica Britannica, 4. London, 1958.

_____, ed. *Music at the Court of Henry VIII*, 2nd ed. Musica Britannica, 18. London, 1969.

Tolkien, J. R. R. and E. V. Gordon. *Sir Gawain and the Green Knight*, 2nd ed., rev. by Norman Davis. Oxford: Clarendon Press, 1968.

Waterhouse, Osborn, ed. *The Non-Cycle Mystery Plays*. EETS, e.s. 114. 1909.

Wilson, H. A. *The Benedictional of Archbishop Robert of Canterbury*. Publications of the Henry Bradshaw Society, 24. 1902.

II. SECONDARY SOURCES

Abraham, Gerald, ed. *The Age of Humanism, 1540-1630*. New Oxford History of Music, IV. London: Oxford Univ. Press, 1968.

Anderson, M. D. *Drama and Imagery in English Medieval Churches.* Cambridge: Cambridge Univ. Press, 1963.

Apel, Willi. *The Notation of Polyphonic Music,* 5th ed. Cambridge: Harvard Univ. Press, 1953.

Bautier Regnier, A.-M. "A Propos des sens de *neuma* et de *nota* en latin médiéval," *Revue belge de musicologie,* 18 (1964), 1-9.

Bayerische Akademie der Wissenschaften und Deutschen Akademie der Wissenschaften zu Berlin. *Mittellateinisches Wörterbuch bis zum ausgehenden 13. Jahrhundert.* Munich, 1959- .

Bent, Margaret. "New and Little-known Fragments of English Medieval Polyphony," *Journal of the American Musicological Society,* 21 (1968), 137-56.

_____. "The transmission of English Music 1300-1500: some aspects of repertory and presentation," in *Studien zur Tradition in der Musik. Kurt von Fischer zum 60. Geburtstag,* ed. Heinrich Eggebrecht and Max Lütolf (Munich: Musikverlag Katzbichler, 1973), pp. 65-83.

Beuscher, Elisabeth. *Die Gesangseinlagen in den englischen Mysterien.* Münster: Helios-Verlag, 1930.

Black, Matthew. *Elizabethan and Seventeenth-Century Lyrics.* Chicago: Lippincott, 1938.

Blomefield, Francis. *An Essay towards a topographical history of the County of Norfolk.* London: Wm. Miller, 1806.

Bolingbroke, Leonard G. "Pre-Elisabethan Plays and Players in Norfolk," *Norfolk Archaeology,* 11 (1892), 332-51.

Bosse, Detlev. *Untersuchung einstimmiger mittelalterlicher Melodien zum "Gloria in Excelsis Deo,"* Forschungsbeiträge zur Musikwissenschaft, 2. Regensburg: G. Bosse, 1955.

Bowles, Edmund A. "*Haut* and *Bas*: The Grouping of Musical Instruments in the Middle Ages," *Musica Disciplina,* 8 (1954), 115-40.

_____. "La Hiérarchie des instruments de musique dans L'Europe féodale," *Revue de musicologie,* 42 (1958), 155-69.

164

_____. "Musical Instruments in civic processions during the Middle Ages," *Acta Musicologica*, 33 (1961), 147-61.

_____. "Musical Instruments in the Medieval Corpus Christi Procession," *Journal of the American Musicological Society*, 17 (1964), 251-60.

_____. "The role of Musical Instruments in Medieval Sacred Drama," *Musical Quarterly*, 45 (1959), 67-84.

_____. "The Symbolism of the Organ in the Middle Ages: A Study in the History of Ideas," in *Aspects of Medieval and Renaissance Music*, ed. Jan LaRue (New York: W. W. Norton, 1966), 27-39.

_____. "Tower Musicians in the Middle Ages," *Brass and Woodwind Quarterly*, 5 (1961-62), 91-103.

_____. "Unterscheidung der Instrumente Buisine, Cor, Trompe und Trompette," *Archiv für Musikwissenschaft*, 18 (1961), 52-72.

Bridge, Joseph C. "The Chester Miracle Plays. . . ," *Journal of the Chester and North Wales Architectural, Archaeological and Historical Society*, 9 (1903), 59-93.

_____. "Three Chester Whitsun Plays," *Journal of the Chester and North Wales Architectural, Archaeological and Historical Society*, 14 (1908), Appendix.

Brown, Carleton, and Rossell Hope Robbins. *The Index of Middle English Verse*. New York: Columbia Univ. Press, 1943.

Bruyne, Edgar de. *Etudes d'esthétique médiéval*. 3 vols. Bruges: De Tempel, 1946.

Bryden, John R., and David G. Hughes. *Index of Gregorian Chant*. 2 vols. Cambridge, Mass.: Harvard Univ. Press, 1969.

Buck, Percy, ed. *Introductory Volume* of the *Oxford History of Music*, 2nd ed. London: Oxford Univ. Press, 1929.

Bukofzer, Manfred. "Speculative Thinking in Medieval Music," *Speculum*, 17 (1942), 165-80.

_____. *Studies in Medieval and Renaissance Music*. New

York: W. W. Norton, 1950; rpt. 1964.

Burch, Clive E. C. *Minstrels and Players in Southampton 1428-1635*. Southampton: Southampton Record Office, 1969.

Butts, Thomas E. "Bagpipes in Medieval Music," *American Recorder*, 14 (1973), 43-45.

Cameron, Kenneth, and Stanley J. Kahrl. "The N-Town Plays at Lincoln," *Theatre Notebook*, 20 (1965-66), 61-69.

Carpenter, Nan Cooke. "Music in the Chester Plays," *Papers on English Language and Literature*, 1 (1965), 195-216.

_____. "Music in the English Mystery Plays," in *Music in English Renaissance Drama*, ed. John H. Long (Lexington: Univ. of Kentucky Press, 1968), pp. 1-31.

_____. "Music in the *Secunda Pastorum*," *Speculum*, 26 (1951), 696-700; rpt. Taylor and Nelson, *Medieval English Drama* (Chicago: Univ. of Chicago Press, 1972), pp. 212-17.

Carter, Henry H. *A Dictionary of Middle English Musical Terms*, ed. George B. Gerhard. Indiana University Humanities Series, 45. Bloomington, 1961; rpt. New York, 1968.

Chambers, E. K. *English Literature at the Close of the Middle Ages*. Oxford History of English Literature, II, 2. Oxf Oxford: Clarendon Press, 1947.

_____. *The Mediaeval Stage*. 2 vols. Oxford: Clarendon Press, 1903.

Clark, Edwin M. "A Restored Reading in the Towneley Purification Play," *Modern Language Notes*, 56 (1941), 358-60.

Collins, Fletcher, Jr. "Music in the Craft Cycles," *PMLA*, 47 (1932), 613-21.

Corbin, Solange. *Essai sur la musique religieuse portugaise au moyen âge*. Paris: Les belles lettres, collection portugaise, 8. 1952.

Craig, Hardin. *English Religious Drama of the Middle Ages*. Oxford: Clarendon Press, 1955.

Cutts, John. "The Second Coventry Carol and a note on *The Maydes Metamorphosis*," *Renaissance News*, 10 (1957), 3-8.

Dent, E. J. "Social Aspects of Music in the Middle Ages," in *Oxford History of Music*, 2nd ed., *Introductory Volume*, ed. P. C. Buck (London: Oxford Univ. Press, 1929), pp. 184-218.

Donovan, Richard B. *The Liturgical Drama in Mediaeval Spain*. Toronto: Pontifical Institute of Mediaeval Studies, 1958.

Du Cange, C. du F., ed. *Glossarium Mediae et infimae Latinitatis*. 10 vols. Niort: Le Favre, 1883-87.

Dutka, JoAnna. "Music and the English Mystery Plays," *Comparative Drama*, 7 (1973), 135-49.

_____. "Mysteries, Minstrels, and Music," *Comparative Drama*, 8 (1974), 112-24; rpt. *Studies in Medieval Drama in Honor of William L. Smoldon* (Kalamazoo, 1974).

_____. *The Use of Music in the English Mystery Plays*. Diss., Univ. of Toronto, 1972.

Forrester, Jean, and A. C. Cawley. "The Corpus Christi Play of Wakefield: A New Look at the Wakefield Burgess Court Records," *Leeds Studies in English*, n.s. 7 (1974), 108-16.

Frere, A. H. and F. W. Galpin. "Shawms and Waits," *Music and Letters*, 4 (1923), 170-77.

Frost, Maurice. *English and Scottish Psalm and Hymn Tunes*. London: SPCK, 1953.

Galpin, Francis. *Old English Instruments of Music*, 4th ed. London: Methuen, 1965.

Gayley, Charles. *Plays of our Forefathers*. London: Chatto and Windus, 1908.

Gifford, Robert M. "The Music and Performance Practices of the Medieval Wind Band," *Journal of Band Research*, 10 (1974), 25-32.

Greene, Richard L. "'The Second Coventry Carol': A Correction," *Renaissance News*, 10 (1957), 142.

Greg, Walter W. *Bibliographical and Textual Problems of the English Miracle Cycles*. London: A. Moring, 1914.

Halle, Edward. *Henry VIII,* ed. Charles Whibley. 2 vols. London: T. C. and E. C. Jack, 1904.

Halliwell-Phillipps, James Orchard. *Outlines of the Life of Shakespeare,* 4th ed. London: Longmans Green, 1884.

Hammerstein, Reinhold. *Die Musik der Engel.* Bern and Munich: Francke, 1962.

Harrison, Frank Lloyd. *Music in Medieval Britain.* London: Routledge and Kegan Paul, 1963.

Hildburgh, W. L. "English Alabaster Carvings as Records of the Medieval Religious Drama," *Archaeologia,* 93 (1949), 51-101.

Hoffman, C. Fenno. "Source of the Words to the Music in York XLVI," *Modern Language Notes,* 65 (1950), 236-39.

Hudson, Frederick. "Robert White and his Contemporaries: Early Elizabethan Music and Drama," in *Festschrift für Ernst Hermann Meyer,* ed. Georg Knepler (Leipzig: Deutscher Verlag für Musik, 1973), pp. 173-87.

Hughes, Dom Anselm, and G. Abraham, eds. *Ars Nova and the Renaissance.* New Oxford History of Music, III. London: Oxford Univ. Press, 1960.

Ingram, R. W. "'To Find the players and all that longeth therto': Notes on the Production of Medieval Drama in Coventry," in *The Elizabethan Theatre V,* ed. G. R. Hibbard (Toronto: Macmillan, 1975), pp. 17-44.

_____. "The use of Music in English Miracle Plays," *Anglia,* 75 (1957), 55-76.

James, M. R. *Catalogue of the Manuscripts in the Library of St. John's College, Cambridge.* Cambridge: Cambridge Univ. Press, 1913.

Kretzmann, Paul E. *The Liturgical Element in the Earliest Forms of the Medieval Drama.* University of Minnesota Studies in Language and Literature, XIV. Minneapolis, 1916.

Kurath, Hans, Sherman M. Kuhn, and John Reidy, eds. *Middle English Dictionary.* Ann Arbor: Univ. of Michigan Press, 1956- .

Latham, R. E., ed. *Revised Medieval Latin Word List*. London: Oxford Univ. Press, 1965.

Le Huray, Peter. *Music and the Reformation in England, 1549-1660*. London: Jenkins, 1967.

Lewis, Charlton T., and Charles Short, eds. *A Latin Dictionary*. Oxford: Clarendon Press, 1879.

Mackerness, Eric D. *A Social History of English Music*. London: Routledge and Kegan Paul, 1964.

Manifold, John S. *Music in English Drama*. London: Rockliff, 1956.

Marcuse, Sybil. *Musical Instruments: A Comprehensive Dictionary*. New York: W. W. Norton, 1975.

Miller, Catherine K. "The Early English Carol," *Renaissance News*, 3 (1950), 61-64.

Moore, J. R. "Miracle Plays, Minstrels, and Jigs," *PMLA*, 48 (1933), 942-45.

_____. "Tradition of Angelic Singing in English Drama," *Journal of English and Germanic Philology*, 22 (1923), 89-99.

Munro, J. "'Tyrly Tirlow' and the Coventry Play of the Nativity," *Notes and Queries*, 11th Series, 1 (1910), 125-26.

Murray, Sir James, *et al.*, eds. *A New English Dictionary on Historical Principles*. 12 vols. Oxford: Clarendon Press, 1888-1928.

Ormerod, George. *A History of the County palatine and City of Chester . . . with a republication of . . . Leycester's Cheshire Antiquities*, ed. Thomas Helsby, 2nd ed. London: Lackington, 1882.

Padelford, Frederick M. *Old English Musical Terms*. Bonner Beiträge zur Anglistik, IV (1899).

Pearson, Lu Emily. "Isolable Lyrics of the Mystery Plays," *ELH*, 3 (1936), 228-52.

Phillips, William J. *Carols, their Origin, Music and Connection with Mystery Plays*. New York: Routledge, 1921.

Reed, Edward B. *Songs from the British Drama*. New Haven: Yale Univ. Press, 1925.

Reese, Gustave. *Music in the Middle Ages*. New York: W. W. Norton, 1940.

_____. *Music in the Renaissance*, rev. ed. New York: W. W. Norton, 1959.

Rimbault, E. F. "An Historical Sketch of the History of Dramatic Music in England," in *Bonduca* by Henry Purcell, ed. E. F. Rimbault. London, 1842.

Ritson, Joseph, ed. *Ancient Songs and Ballads*. 2 vols. London: Payne and Foss, 1829.

Robbins, Rossell Hope, and John L. Cutler. *Supplement to the Index of Middle English Verse*. Lexington: Univ. of Kentucky, 1965.

Rokseth, Yvonne. "Une source peu étudiée d'iconographie musicale," *Revue de musicologie*, 14 (1933), 74-85.

Rossiter, A. P. *English Drama from Early Times to the Elizabethans*. London: Hutchinson, 1950.

Sachs, Curt. *Real-Lexicon der Musikinstrumente*. 1913; rpt. New York: Dover, 1964.

Salter, F. M. "The Banns of the Chester Plays," *Review of English Studies*, 15 (1939), 432-57; 16 (1940), 1-17 and 137-48.

Salter, Frederick M. *Mediaeval Drama in Chester*. 1955; rpt. New York: Russell and Russell, 1968.

_____. "The Trial & Flagellation: A New Manuscript," *The Trial & Flagellation with Other Studies in the Chester Cycle*, ed. W. W. Greg. Malone Society Studies (Oxford, 1935), pp. 1-73.

Schad, Gustav. *Musik und Musikausdrücke in der mittelenglischen Literatur*. Frankfort-am-Mainz: H. Richter, 1911.

Schuler, Ernst A. *Die Musik der Osterfeiern, Osterspiele und*

Passionen des Mittelalters. Kassel and Basel: Bärenreiter, 1951.

Smits Van Waesberghe, Joseph. *Cymbala (Bells in the Middle
Ages)*. Musicological Studies and Documents, I. Rome:
American Institute of Musicology, 1951.

Smoldon, W. L. "Medieval Church Drama and the Use of Musical
Instruments," *Musical Times*, 103 (1962), 836-40.

Spencer, Matthew L. *Corpus Christi Pageants in England*. New
York: Baker and Taylor, 1911.

Stephen, George A. "The Waits of the City of Norwich," *Norfolk
Archaeology*, 25 (1935), 1-70.

Stevens, John. "Carols and Court Songs of the Early Tudor Period," *Proceedings of the Royal Musical Association*, 77
(1951), 51-62.

_____. *Music and Poetry in the Early Tudor Court*. London:
Methuen, 1961.

_____. "Music in Medieval Drama," *Proceedings of the Royal
Musical Association*, 84 (1957-58), 81-95.

Stevens, Martin. "Language as Theme in the Wakefield Plays,"
Speculum, 52 (1977), 100-17.

Stratman, Carl J. *Bibliography of Medieval Drama*. Berkeley,
1954; 2nd ed., New York: Ungar, 1972.

Taylor, Jerome, and Alan H. Nelson, eds. *Medieval English
Drama: Essays Critical and Contextual*. Chicago: Univ. of
Chicago Press, 1972.

Traver, Hope. "Relation of Musical Terms in the Woodkirk Shepherds Plays to the Date of Their Composition," *Modern Language Notes*, 20 (1905), 1-5.

Vriend, Joannes. *The Blessed Virgin Mary in the Medieval Drama
of England*. Purmerend: Muusses, 1928.

Walker, Ernest. *A History of Music in England*, 3rd ed. Oxford:
Clarendon Press, 1952.

Wall, Carolyn. "York Pageant XLVI and its Music (with a Note on the Transcriptions by Ruth Steiner)," *Speculum*, 46 (1971), 689-712.

Wall, Sister Catherine. *A Study of "The Appearance of Our Lady To Thomas." Pageant XLVI in the York Cycle of Mystery Plays*. Diss., Catholic University of America, 1965.

Wilson, F. P. *The English Drama, 1485-1585*, ed. G. K. Hunter. Oxford History of English Literature, IV, 1. Oxford: Clarendon Press, 1969.

Withington, Robert. *English Pageantry*. 2 vols. Cambridge, Mass.: Harvard Univ. Press, 1918-20.

_____. "Thre Brefes to a Long," *Modern Language Notes*, 18 (1943), 115-16.

Wolf, J. "Anonymi cujusdam Codex Basiliensis," *Vierteljahrsschrift für Musikwissenschaft*, 9 (1893), 408-17.

Woodfill, Walter L. *Musicians in English Society*. Princeton: Princeton Univ. Press, 1963; rpt. New York, 1969.

Wooldridge, H. O., ed. *The Oxford History of Music,* 2nd ed. rev. by Percy Buck. Vols. I and II. London: Oxford Univ. Press, 1929-32.

Wordsworth, Christopher. *Ceremonies and Processions of the Cathedral Church of Salisbury*. Cambridge: Cambridge Univ. Press, 1901.

Young, Karl. *The Drama of the Medieval Church*. 2 vols. Oxford: Clarendon Press, 1933.